TAKING POSITIONS
IN THE ORGANIZATION

Other titles in the
Systemic Thinking and Practice Series
edited by David Campbell & Ros Draper
published and distributed by Karnac

Credit Card orders, Tel: +44 (0) 20-8969-4454; Fax: +44 (0) 20-8969-5585
Email: shop@karnacbooks.com

TAKING POSITIONS
IN THE ORGANIZATION

David Campbell
Marianne Grønbæk

Foreword by
Rom Harré

Systemic Thinking and Practice Series

Series Editors
David Campbell & Ros Draper

KARNAC
LONDON   NEW YORK

First published in 2006 by
H. Karnac (Books) Ltd.
118 Finchley Road, London NW3 5HT

British Library Cataloguing in Publication Data

A C.I.P. for this book is available from the British Library

ISBN: 978-1-85575-384-6

Edited, designed, and produced by Communication Crafts

Printed by the MPG Books Group, Bodmin and King's Lynn

www.karnacbooks.com

CONTENTS

SERIES EDITORS' FOREWORD

It seems appropriate for this book to consider its own position in the fields of both systemic thinking and work with organizations. Regarding the former, the book represents a new development of social constructionist thinking. It explores the way broad societal and organizational discourses offer specific positions from which we construct, through dialogue, the day-to-day realities that govern our behaviour in organizations. One central premise is that organizations change when we shift our personal positions, and we can only shift our positions through dialogue with other people in other positions.

Within the field of organizational work, the book addresses one aspect of a manager's job—that is, creating reflective space for people to observe themselves and others operating in the workplace. Managers certainly need to manage, direct, control, and evaluate processes, but in order to generate new ideas and new working relationships, they also need to involve their staff in a process of creating space away from the daily work where new ideas lead to new practices. This is a book that offers a clear and well-developed method for doing just that.

The book is based on David Campbell's and Marianne Grønbæk's years of experience as organization consultants. It is therefore rich in application and rich in the variety of working contexts exposed to this model. The authors have given space to present the voice of those who have used this model: what has been helpful to them and what has not. And more importantly, has this model made a difference to the way people feel about themselves and their work?

The authors are also interested in training others to use this model within their own organizational work, therefore the ideas and techniques are presented clearly and concisely and there are numerous exercises to help groups take on this model themselves. The book is a fascinating read from both the theoretical and applied perspectives and will be engaging for readers who want to apply the ideas to therapeutic settings as well as organizational ones.

David Campbell
Ros Draper
London, February 2006

ABOUT THE AUTHORS

David Campbell is an established clinical psychologist and works as a trainer and clinician for the National Health Service at the Tavistock Clinic in London and also as a freelance consultant to teams and small organizations. In his work with organizations, he has been interested for many years in developing techniques that incorporate the principles of systemic thinking. His work has led to consulting and training projects throughout the United Kingdom and Europe, for both public and private sector institutions. He has written several articles and books on this subject and is co-editor of the Systemic Thinking and Practice Series, containing 39 books, which has promoted many new ideas in this field.

Marianne Grønbæk is an organizational consultant with a background in family therapy and management. Since 1997 she has been the manager of MG-UDVIKLING, a successful consulting firm offering consultation, supervision, and education to managers and employees in private and public organizations in Denmark and Scandinavia. She is a practice-centred consultant, and her particular interest is in working with organizations to create models of organization and communication that lead to better practice. Her work is inspired by systemic thinking, appreciative practice, Positioning theory, and Semantic Polarities, and she has recently published a book, *Drommen—fra tanke til handling* [The Dream—From Idea to Action], about the use of appreciative inquiry in her consultation work.

Rom Harré began his career in mathematics and physics, moving through the philosophy of science to work in the foundations of psychology. He is Emeritus Fellow of Linacre College, Oxford, and currently teaches in Washington, DC, at both Georgetown University and American University.

FOREWORD

Rom Harré

The study of social interactions was very slow to cast off the presuppositions of the behaviourist era in psychology. In the prevailing picture that dominated research for much of the twentieth century, it was presumed that social phenomena resulted from individuals coming together with permanent and established attributes. Their patterns of interaction were presumed to be responses to externally imposed stimuli. This was the era of attitude research and of the study of attitude change by reference to individual feelings of cognitive dissonance. The role of speech and other symbolic exchanges was left to sociologists and linguists to unravel. Methodology was confined to simple experiments in which complex social phenomena were dissected into independent and dependent variables, without any attention to the structures from which they were abstracted. The upshot of all this was an impoverished and unrealistic picture of how people created social life. It is scarcely surprising that there was little of use to practical people, whether they were dealing with psychiatric problems of individuals or with malfunctioning institutions such as businesses, governmental departments, and so on.

Gradually, starting in the 1970s, a very different paradigm began to emerge. Three main principles crystallized out of a multitude of scattered researches. First of all, it became clear that social life consisted not of isolated encounters but of unfolding episodes, the structures of which were more important in explanatory terms than any alleged attributes that the interactors brought to the encounter. This idea was neatly summed up by Erving Goffman in the epigram "Not men and their moments, but moments and their men". Equally revolutionary was the realization that most social encounters are symbolic and, in particular, occur through the medium of language. Social life is literally a conversation. Discourse conventions, narratives, or story lines, not causal mechanisms, determine how relationships unfold. Instead of experiments, the cutting edge of social psychology turned to the recording and analysis of actual encounters and the means whereby meanings were maintained and managed. The last piece of the jigsaw that completed the new picture was the realization that social life was dominated by ever-changing moral demands. People very often did what they did because of their convictions as to what were their rights and what duties were required of them. Where did these convictions come from? Frequently the moral demands of particular episodes were as much imposed by the social order in which a strip of life was unfolding as they were the result of the beliefs of the individual persons engaged in them.

It is important to realize just how radical the new paradigm of social life as conversation actually is. Most importantly, it involves the abandonment of thinking in terms of causality. Instead, one thinks in terms of rules, conventions, and—above all—relations between meanings as the organizing principles of social encounters. The research project then shifts from looking for causal relations to extricating meanings and the rules and conventions for their management.

In the last few years of the twentieth century, the importance of attending to the moral implications of ways of acting and the shifting basis for these in real life led to the development of a new research style: "Positioning theory". A position is a cluster of duties and rights, with various associated psychological matters such as emotions and relevant skills. Positions are available in micro-cultures, the members of which can come to take up positions, reject and abandon positions, contest positions, and so on. Positions are relative to other positions, so Positioning theory is a version of the constructionist paradigm and maintains the necessity of seeing the life of human beings in structural and systemic terms. Positions appear as much in talk as in action. In either mode, unravelling them depends on focusing on the meanings not only of what is said, but also on what is done.

The authors of this book, David Campbell and Marianne Grønbæk, seem to me to have made two major contributions to new paradigm psychology and Positioning theory and to have enhanced its practicability at the same time. The first is their notion of "semantic polarity", which makes it possible to accept and make a virtue of the postmodernist insistence that formal contradiction is a prevailing feature of human life. This enables the creation and occupancy of new positions in which the dilemmas that express the formal contradictions of belief and practice that might prove fatal to the maintenance of a successful form of life are used as springboards towards fruitful repositionings. The importance of choice of polarities as determining the possibilities and content of repositionings comes out very well in the numerous case studies provided with this book.

The use of "Positioning theory" in all sorts of studies—from the intricacies of courtroom battles, through environmentalist debates, to military chains of command—has been at the mercy of clever intuitions. The authors' second major contribution is that they have given us a structured programme for conducting practical studies in organizations and other social communities around the dilemmas that provoke positionings, whether malign or benign. They show how the work of the consultant, using their fivefold schema, can ensure that benign repositionings can be promoted and the destructive dilemmas turned to beneficent use and eventually transcended as new patterns of positions are encouraged.

There are other invaluable refinements to Positioning theory in this book. For example, "power"—a crucial sociological variable—is defined in Positioning theory terms. Like Foucault, the authors also see power in linguistic terms, leading to the idea of safe and dangerous conversations. This distinction is implicit in many Positioning theory studies but has hitherto lacked explicit formulation. Perhaps the "practice" orientation of this book would privilege safe over dangerous conversational styles.

Of greater importance for Positioning theory generally, Campbell and Grønbæk have made the process of repositioning more explicit in introducing the idea of transcendent positions. The nature of a conflict can be expressed in terms of polarized positions, but if the practical work of the consultant is confined to attempts to reconcile or even choose between such positions, there is little hope of resolution, as has been shown in any number of studies of conflict analysed in positioning terms. A transcendent position, from which the contradictory positions can be viewed, makes possible the transformation of first-order dialogue into second-order dialectic, facilitating radical repositionings. This suggests the importance of the choice of polarity that a consultant might make to begin the transformation of the scene.

The book is rich in practical illustrations through which the virtues of the research schema and the ways it can be implemented are made evident. Every step of the way is associated with a case history, so that the abstractions of the leading concepts—"Semantic Polarities" and "Positions"—are grounded in concrete instances. One whole chapter is devoted to exercises through which the practical work of choosing polarities and the positions that they implicate can be learned.

What we have here is a work with a double import. On the one hand, as I have emphasized, there are all sorts of contributions to the development of Positioning theory, refining and amplifying many central aspects of that style of new paradigm psychology. On the other hand, here is a practical manual, with step-by-step advice on how to bring positioning analysis to life in the work of the consultant. The authors are wary of making extravagant claims for their working practices, qualifying each piece of advice with the need to take account of the particularities of the situations with which they are engaged. Both consultant and client have their chances to voice the view from each subjective position.

This is an important book, not only from the point of view of advancing Positioning theory, but also by the strength and practicality of its methodology in the consultation process itself.

CHAPTER ONE

Introduction

Picture a seminar with twenty students. While one of the authors (MG) was presenting the Semantic Polarities model to them, a student suddenly interrupted, saying: "It's not possible to use Semantic Polarities all the time."

The group went silent, and all eyes were on me to see how I would respond. I felt stuck, and I wondered to myself why he was saying this now, when things were going well—he was spoiling everything. I said to him, "I could ask you to be quiet and get on with the exercise, or I could ask you to hold on to your point of view and I will take the opposite position."

He tried to negotiate a bit by saying, "I only said what I did because you had implied that this model could be used all the time," but my response was: "No, you stick to your position and your statement and I will stick to mine, and we will invite the rest of the group to discuss these positions as two ends of a polarity." I also thought it was important to take this seriously, and I thanked him for creating the opportunity to work on this polarity.

I went to the whiteboard and drew the polarity like this:

MG   Student

|——|

Semantic Polarities   Semantic Polarities
can be used with any problem   cannot always be used

Then I asked the other students to draw this polarity, position themselves somewhere on the line, and discuss in groups of three what was good about each position. We ended this diversion with a general discussion, and the student reported that he felt that his challenging statement was acceptable.

The book

This book is about people in organizations. It is about how they see the world and how they talk to each other. And it is about how they create a view of themselves and the organization through these conversations.

We are two consultants who have developed a model for working with people in organizations, helping them to resolve dilemmas and develop constructive working relationships by changing the way they see and talk to colleagues. We have found over the years that this model is effective and popular with clients, and our purpose in writing this book is to share our experience and widen the use of these ideas to include people working within an organization as well as the external consultant.

The book is written for anyone seeking a model for helping people move away from stuck positions and difficult relationships in the workplace. It will be helpful for consultants who have a remit to address organizational problems or to increase productivity, and it will be helpful to managers who are trying to inspire individuals and who work with staff relations on a daily basis. We have also been pleasantly surprised by how much employees themselves have taken to these ideas by, for example, building them into structured discussions during team meetings. The model offers simple ideas that can gradually impact on complex processes.

Our primary aim as consultants is for people to think differently about themselves and others in the organization, and this inevitably leads to seeing new possibilities for action in the workplace. The model we are going to explore in this book is a means to reaching this end. It is a way of enabling people to see their behaviour as one position among many, with the potential to change along with the changing positions of others in the organization. Our aim is neither prescriptive nor specific, other than our intention that people feel freer, more creative, and able to have different types of interactions with their colleagues and managers.

The title of the book, *Taking Positions in the Organization*, was chosen because this is a familiar process we can all identify with, but the title is also meant to lure the reader into a more complex model of organizational behaviour based on the concept of Semantic Polarities that is thoroughly explored in this volume. In fact, we refer to our model throughout the book as the Semantic Polarities model.

We shall be writing about creating realities through dialogue and the risks of closing down conversation through expertise and certainty, but the one thing we would not prescribe is putting things in writing—they can begin to look like realities. It is a challenge to convey the tension, excitement, and frustration of sitting and working with a group of colleagues in the workplace, but writing about it, as we do in this book, is an exercise in freezing the ongoing process, thereby creating an artificial reality. However, this is exactly what we argue against, so it is frustrating. On the other hand, if we look at the book as the first half of a dialogue with the reader, and leave it at that—this will free us up to get on with the job and leave the rest to you.

Interestingly, although as authors we created this book together, so far we have never worked together with clients. We met at various seminars and training events and almost by accident discovered that we were enamoured of the same ideas and were working in similar ways, but in different countries. Though still getting to know each other, there is a mutual fascination with this model we describe. We have decided to publish this book simultaneously in English and Danish* to reach constituents and interested readers in many parts of the world.

Because of this, we need to introduce ourselves to each other as much as to our reading audience. We believe it is important to acknowledge who we are as people and to say something about how we use ourselves and our own biases in our work. This may help us and the reader take account of our own positions as we describe our work. Therefore, we have each made a personal statement to get this book under way.

David

I came into this work through a clinical psychology training at Boston University, in the United States. I moved to London in 1972 and became interested in the National Health Service as an organization that maintained a value-based service of free care for all citizens, an organization that was also one of the largest in the world (apparently rivalled in size only by the Indian Railway and the Russian Army). About the time I was trying to establish myself as a clinician and identify myself with a model I could call my own, I discovered the systemic model for conducting family therapy sessions. This awakened me to a world of interaction between people which could, on the one hand, generate serious mental health problems but also, on the other, had the potential to release these problems by creating new patterns of interaction.

In my role as a psychologist, I was frequently asked to provide some form of consultation to small working teams or residential units, and I found that the systemic ideas I used in the clinical setting fitted perfectly into my work with organizations. Organizations were nothing if not systems, and the systemic model provided ways that I could identify the interaction between the parts and the struggle to create common meaning from disparate points of view in the workplace (see Campbell, Draper, & Huffington, 1991; Campbell, Coldicott, & Kinsella,

---

*M. Grønbæk & D. Campbell, *Semantiske Polariteter og Positioner: Samtaler i organisationer* (Denmark: MG-UDVIKLING, 2005).

1994). I first met Marianne at a seminar when we were trying to apply systemic thinking to organizational consultation.

But why have the ideas described in this book—those of Semantic Polarities and Positioning theory—become so compelling to me? I grew up as the younger of two brothers, born after a five-year gap, with the experience of having arrived into a ready-made family preceded by a brother who seemed to already occupy an important place in family life. As I look at this from my adult perspective, it seems that he was acknowledged as the one who would be well-behaved and who would inevitably get things right, and this appeared to be very important to my parents. I didn't understand why at the time, but it did seem like this was an "occupied position"—position not vacant, applicants need not apply. So now I can see how this process fascinates me. Perhaps it is my effort to understand how all this positioning works because it seemed to have been worked out before my arrival on the scene, and perhaps it is also an attempt to find my position and have it recognized and valued.

Another aspect of positioning that intrigues me is its potential for creating a "level playing-field"—that is, everyone is equal in the sense that everyone can be construed to occupy a position within the same discourse. That is a good starting point. The subsequent attribution of goodness and badness to certain positions can be understood not as internal states but as the result of further workings of other heretofore undisclosed discourses. This is very freeing because an individual's actions can be externalized and given meaning in other contexts. So, as the new arrival in my family, I see the value of everyone being treated equally to a position within a family discourse.

I see semantic polarities as the sites within the discourses where meanings are negotiated, and, in a similar vein, I have been motivated as a younger sibling to make meanings on an equal basis with the others in the family. I must have asked myself hundreds of times, "What do things mean" and "How does this all work?" Today, with the model of Semantic Polarities, I have a chance to find out. I feel that Semantic Polarities take me to the heart of the process of making meaning.

Now, in my practice as a consultant, I value being able to get close to people's experience, to feel some of what others feel;

however, I also need to be able to step back and see the larger pattern, or the process, of the interacting individuals. How do I find a position that gives me the right degree of closeness and distance? The question I ask myself is: "Where do I position my 'self' when using this model of consultation?" One answer would be that I occupy a position called "consultant" within an organization's discourse about external helpers. The meaning given to the position and the way I am positioned by the employees will determine how they respond to me and what feelings are stirred up in me when I am in that position. I can use these feelings to understand something about how I am positioned and what this may mean for the organization, and, in fact, I may choose to verbally comment on what I am feeling in order to invite or position others within the "feeling" discourse.

So another answer to the question might be that when I respond by bringing my self into the discussion, by, for example, saying, "This is what I feel at this moment", I am choosing to take a position within a "feeling" discourse and inviting others to take a position in relation to mine. For example, others may be invited to agree or disagree with my feeling or reflect on their own feelings at that moment. So my choice as a consultant is to decide which would be the most helpful discourse to call forth as I introduce my "self" and my own ideas into the discussion. A consultant can never be unbiased or value-free, but he or she can take decisions that direct the conversation towards particular discourses in the organization.

If someone were to ask me, "How do you feel when you sit in this group" (as I have been asked on many occasions), I might say how I do feel sitting with them, or, alternatively, I might choose to ask if this is an important theme for others in the group. In either case, I would try to keep in mind that a discourse about feelings or a discourse about personal reflections from an external helper is being summoned and that whatever I say invites people to take positions, so I will try to follow the way new positions are taken and be curious about the meaning that these discourses have for the group.

During my second meeting with Marianne, at another seminar, in which we discovered quite by chance that we were both fascinated with this way of thinking and with the model of Semantic Polarities. We had each been "beavering-away" on our own, putting these ideas into action. A few years later she sent an email asking if I was interested in collaborating with her on a book about our work—and this is the result!

Marianne

Why systemic therapy? Why Semantic Polarities? Why speculate about positions? Well, at this point it would sound very streamlined to maintain that in my case it was a straightforward, strategic choice. I have to disappoint those of you who like streamlined statements. My choices seem to be made at random—but what does that "at random" imply ? All three abovementioned questions can be answered from the heart: because they work for me. Because they make sense to me. Because they give me the freedom to think. So maybe it is a straightforward, strategic choice on the one hand, and a spontaneous choice from the heart on the other.

In my earliest years as a family therapist, I was working in a children's counselling clinic. The social security office that sent clients to us were satisfied with the result of therapy we gave them but not with the relatively small number of clients we were able to treat. Therefore, the townships wanted to close down the clinic and spend the money instead on locally based counselling. As therapists we wanted to stay together because, among other things, we highly valued how our various professional skills complemented each other. So instead of allowing ourselves to be closed down, we put forward a plan to the county politicians: we intended to increase the number of families in therapy substantially. But how?

Luckily there were some fresh winds blowing across Denmark: systemic family therapy and brief solution-focused family therapy. We took the chance and went to seminars conducted by Gianfranco Cecchin and Steve de Shazer, which proved to be crucial and very provocative experiences for us. It was quite an opposite way of thinking—*but* it fulfilled our demands of working "faster". The method offered us the opportunity of talking to the whole family at once and to call in all the relations. The method seemed to me to be more energizing than the methods I had previously worked with. This was the way I was introduced to the systemic method, which I found gave me the space to "play" more. I liked being able to incorporate the families in their own solutions to their own problems. I felt that this way of thinking lifted the atmosphere in the therapy-room.

In relation to my family background, the systemic way of thinking seems to fit in very well. I am the third out of four sisters, all born within the course of five years. Our house was a very open one, and my parents were helpful to a great number of people. There were always many people around, and it seemed to a child like me that you had to be able to find your own place(s). And you had to relate to a lot of different people in different ways. With four daughters, the kitchen and my mother's skirts were taken. I became my father's girl, and I spent time playing with him and following his activities inside and outside our home. I was introduced to a lot of people, some like-minded as well as others who thought differently. I got a lot of insight into how other people were living with their families, and I soon felt it was natural to "play" with positions.

I chose a career as a social worker. I wanted to see justice done. But after working in that profession for three years, I felt the need for something different. In those three years of social work, I had discovered that my clients covered three genera-tions of the same family. It made me think that we had to change our approach and our ways of thinking. This is when I started searching for "what works". Ever since, I have been concerned about finding new ways that are effective, and I have been very critical of the numerous fancy initiatives that are not.

Many years ago I joined a systemic supervision training group, with David as instructor, and saw how he did what I valued so highly: looking for what works for the individual, in a simple and very appreciative way. His way of listening to and guiding the individual participant was an experience that left its mark on me. It made everyone a master of her or his own situation.

Since 1995 I have been working as a consultant in organiza-tions and since 1998 within the framework of my own firm

(Grønbæk, 2004). In 1998 I went to a seminar that introduced me to the model of Appreciative Inquiry (Cooperrider & Srivastra, 1987). I felt that the thinking was useful for me in my work and started using it in my own way. In 2000 I attended an Appreciative Inquiry seminar run by Peter Lang from the KCC Foundation. This way of thinking felt natural to me, and I discovered that it was the way my life had been, the way my father had raised me. It was a very special experience as my father had died only two weeks earlier. I felt that this was the widest polarity in my life so far: my father's death and the *joie de vivre* expressed through Appreciative Inquiry.

In the spring of 2001 I attended a seminar with David. He invited all participants to work with and develop a new method that he called Semantic Polarities. I knew of David's way of leading people through a learning process, so I left it to him to guide me through the unknown territory. And the further I got, the more sense it made and the more brilliantly it felt. David maintained that differences were necessary for development! It made sense to me as a human being, considering my background. I felt the broad, free space it created. I discovered the answers to the difficult questions I had met with within Appreciative Inquiry: how to handle oppositions, disagreements, and differences in a way that felt helpful and effective for the persons involved and made them feel that their difficulties were appreciated and taken seriously. In fact, Semantic Polarities and the understanding of positions gave me the feeling of being able to play even more freely. Or, phrased in a more professional way: Semantic Polarities made it possible to use conflicts, and disagreements, for development.

It made me think back. In my family it was impossible for my parents to take all the children's pranks seriously—there would not have been time for anything else if they had. Humour was often used by us girls and by our parents. My father's office was a part of our home, so he took part in the bringing up of his children. Even in his busy everyday life, he often dealt with our conflicts. He had a brilliant way of solving them: he would ask us to stand face to face and look into each other's eyes, and, of course, it did not take long before we couldn't help laughing. Due to his mediation we had no other opportunity than to "relate to the position of the other party". Without knowing the term, he adopted "Position C" (which will be discussed later). I am sure he knew what it would mean to the conflict were he to favour one child over the other. And we felt his warm and genuine interest in us, not in the conflict.

Why, then, "positions" and "semantic polarities"? By looking at our own and other peoples' positions, a playground is created in which we can relate to the things that really matter to us. We need not explain it in many words. We are allowed just to exist in the moments that are important to us. You might say that by doing so, you move from your head to your heart. And actions of the heart are very simple and powerful. The process of writing this book has made it even clearer to me how these methods can be applied strategically, for the benefit of managers, consultants, and all members of staff, in any kind of organization.

When you work with positions, you work with the relations between these positions and the way the positions influence each other. This process means a lot to people. To be a part of meaningful processes is precious to me. I often tell my clients that my life is important in all aspects. Therefore, I want everything that I do to be important and meaningful—to me as well as to the people with whom I work.

Our biases

We have identified several values that influence our thinking and have inevitably influenced the way we describe our model and discuss our work in this book.

Foremost is our commitment to a social constructionist view of the world, which means that rather than attributing the source of our behaviour to individual, internal factors such as attitudes, emotional states, or personality, we take the view that our sense of who we are and how we want to behave results from the positions we choose, and are given, within the range of discourses that society offers us. We generate the meanings that guide our behaviour through conversation with others who have also taken specific positions within particular discourses.

The way we function in organizations depends partly on what we bring as individuals and partly on the way the organization places individuals in positions that have accompanying rights, duties, and responsibilities.

We believe in the power of dialogue to create realities and then in changing them when they seem to be unhelpful. This means we would subscribe to Riikonen's (1999) definition of a problem as an "activity which is outside dialogue".

Writing this book has led us to re-examine one of our central values—that when a method is defined and pinned down, its ability to adapt and develop in response to its changing environment is put at risk—so rather than specifying a particular method, we prefer to equip the reader with a range of ideas and accounts of how we have applied them in different ways and different situations.

Against method

Users of a method may easily find themselves preoccupied by the mistakes they make and in correcting each other as they try to get back on the road. The discussions about the method will often amount to whether this or that is "correct" according to the described method.

I (MG) remember an episode in 1985 when I attended a seminar run by Steve de Shazer from Milwaukee. One of the participants commented on a difference between what Steve had taught at a previous seminar and what he was saying at this one. The difference was that Steve had originally said that all relevant persons should be invited to family therapy, yet here we were watching a video-recording in which there was only one person in the therapy session. The participant asked Steve why he no longer did what he had previously said and done. At the same time he said that in their clinic they tried to follow strictly what Steve had previously taught. Steve did not want to talk about what he used to do—he preferred to talk about the advantages of the method he used currently. The participant got very angry with Steve, who persisted in talking about what he was doing now and what worked well about it. The participant got even angrier, and Steve said that he could regard it as a development of the method. The participant got up and left the seminar. Some of the participants thought that Steve was being rude, whereas others found that the fact that the "master" himself maintained the right to change and develop gave them a great feeling of freedom: if he can do it, so can we.

As we have developed our ideas about positioning and the creation of meaning within Semantic Polarities, we have learned much from those situations where things did not work out. We have also experienced how the same kind of methods have been trammels to the very development of ideas and thus limited creativity and new ideas. To some of the members of an organization, the method is seen as a good and safe framework for development: their energy is concentrated entirely on "learning" the method. To other members of the same organization, the framework feels too narrow and seems to prevent development: such members may rightfully say that the method has given them the feeling of "being taught". Winston Churchill once said:

I am always ready to learn—
But I am not always ready to be taught.

CHAPTER TWO

Ideas that underpin the model

This book represents a convergence of three streams of thought that are broadly informed by systemic thinking and social constructionism. These are: Discourse theory and Semantic Polarities; Positioning theory; and Dialogue theory.

They have been pulled together to create a model for understanding and working with organizations from the position of the insider—that is, the manager—or the outsider—that is, the consultant.

The aim of this method is to assist people in their working environment to understand why they and their colleagues behave as they do and to enable them to create a conversation with others that will help them shift their thinking and behaviour.

Discourse

The method begins with Discourse Theory and Semantic Polarities. This proposes that we all make sense of the world—and decide how to act—by taking a position within a range of meanings about ourselves and our environment. These different meanings are offered to us in the form of discourses generated at many levels of our social experience. For example, our society generates a discourse about "globalization"; our workplace generates a discourse about good governance; and our family generates a discourse about sharing with others. We can take one of many positions that are available within these specific discourses.

One definition of a discourse is an institutionalized use of language and language-like sign systems, which can occur at many levels such as the cultural, political, or organizational. Discourses occur around specific topics such as gender, class, or power. "Discourses can compete with each other or they can create distinct and incompatible versions of reality. To know anything is to know in terms of one or more discourses" (Harré & Langenhove, 1999). This means that our experience of working in an organization can only be expressed and understood through the categories available to us in the discourses that are generated by the organization itself.

Discourses offer a number of subject positions that give the individual two things: a framework for understanding the organization, known as the "conceptual repertoire"; and a location for a person that stipulates the rights, duties, and behaviours possible for people using that particular repertoire.

Davies and Harré (1990) put it neatly when they say,

> Who one is, that is what sort of person one is, is always an open question with a shifting answer depending upon the positions made available within one's own and others' discursive practices, and within those practices, the stories through which we make sense of our own and others' lives. Stories are located within a number of discourses and thus vary dramatically in terms of the language used, the concepts, issues and moral judgments made relevant, and the subject positions made available within them. [p. 35]

Semantic Polarities

These different positions can be placed on one continuum, or what we call a semantic polarity—*semantic* because it provides the basis for meaning. The theory was originally introduced into clinical practice by Ugazio (1998), who studied the semantic polarities operating in families with phobic, obsessive compulsive, and eating disorders. The formulation of a construct that acquires its meaning through the interplay of contrasting or opposing positions is also the basis of Kelly's (1955) Personal Construct theory, which was developed in the United Kingdom by Bannister (1970) and others. However, our model applies these ideas to the organizational context, and one example of how we might do this would be as follows.

> Imagine an organization that strives to maintain two important values in its work: meanings about providing a quality service and meanings about saving money. These two values within the organization can be positioned at two opposite poles. At one pole the position is represented by a value statement, "The priority for this organization is to cut costs"; at the other pole is the position represented by the statement, "The organization must maintain the quality of our service regardless of cost." Once the pole positions have been clarified, there is the potential to create many intermediate positions between the poles. So, for example, an intermediate position might be "We will try to cut our costs by 20%" or "We can reduce the quality a bit by working in a different way".

| Cut costs | Cut costs by 20% | | Reduce quality a bit | Maintain quality |

> Scaling technique then allows us to place a range of statement on the continuum, each representing a different position in the "cost vs. quality" polarity.

Organizational culture and meaning

Each organization, large or small, will build a culture upon a number of these semantic polarities that are necessary to generate meaning about what the organization stands for and how to act within the organizational context. They define the culture of the organization and help everyone answer the question, "How should I act?" Other examples of organizational polarities are: (1) In an organization in which the culture values the individual contribution of its workers, the polarity will be complete independence at one end and complete adherence to collaboration at the other, and all the positions in between: "Workers should be independent" and "Workers should work together for the sake of the whole". (2) In another organization in which the culture values loyalty, the polarity may be: "Complete loyalty to management" at one end and "Total disloyalty" at the other.

The point is that once we can identify the values within the culture of the organization, and the different discourses that express the values, we can place the values within a range of positions along a polarity. The act of taking one position along a polarity among other positions is the act of creating meaning for ourselves and others. Meaning does not arise independent of this positioning process. It is the stretching of the polarity to its extremes that allows us to imagine the many positions in between. In this way, meaning becomes a relative concept because our ideas or our behaviour must be compared to other positions along a polarity to become meaningful. This is the first step in the process: *identifying the values within the organization and placing them within a polarity.*

Taking a position

The next step is underpinned by Positioning theory (Langenhove & Harré, 1999). Generally, we choose to take positions within discourses, and we are also positioned by others on the basis of what we say and do. Davies and Harré (1990) refer to these types of positioning as *"interactive positioning* in which what one person says positions another, and there can be *reflexive positioning* in which one positions oneself" (p. 37); emphasis added). Let's take an example from the everyday working world:

> Employee A walks up to Employee B and says, "I thought you were going to send this report to Mary Jones". Now,

if Speaker B treats this remark as a criticism, he feels positioned as someone who has done something wrong—a position he may not want to accept—and he therefore positions A as "a criticizing person". From this position, and the position assigned to A, Employee B may now reply defensively, "Why didn't you make it more clear to me who the report should be sent to?" Now Speaker A has been positioned as someone who has made a mistake—a position that he, likewise, may not want to accept—and therefore he responds by saying, "I did make it clear, you weren't listening carefully . . .". And so on and so on.

We are, then, invited to take a position within the range that is offered, but we are also simultaneously being positioned by other people in the organization. Positioning theory makes the point that each position is defined by the others along the continuum. So this means, I will see myself on a certain position as a "loyal colleague" on the loyalty polarity, but I only know the position I take—and I can only understand my own sense of loyalty—by looking around and seeing that there are other positions that represent different versions of loyalty from my own. In other words, I know that I am loyal if I can see, or imagine, less loyal colleagues around me. In fact, we probably need a sense that some people are more loyal and some are less loyal, and we can imagine spreading these people across a continuum of many different degrees of loyalty.

Harré and Moghaddam (2004) put it like this:

Positions are relative to one another. If one is positioned as "nurse", the expectation will be that someone else will be positioned as "patient". Even taking on the nurse position oneself may serve to position someone else as patient whether he or she did or did not want it. Often someone positioning himself/herself as patient drives someone else into the nurse position. It is easy to see that these positions are nothing but clusters of rights, duties, and obligations to perform, or to require the performance of certain acts (from others). In psychological reality, positions exist as expectations, beliefs and presuppositions. [p. 6]

Being positioned

The process of being positioned by others is complicated, but it is crucial to our understanding of how organizations work. In order to take a position and maintain it with its attached emotions and values and status, I need to place others in positions relative to mine. Deetz (2003) described the reciprocal process in terms of the development of identity, which is never simply a "self process": "Becoming a subject is always a subjugation as well as a move of agency and subjugates as well as gives particular agency to others" (p. 126).

In a sense, the others "prop me up" (or prop me down!) in my position. When I do this I create a "position-pair". Examples of this would be statements such as: "She is not as interested in this work as I am" (meaning, I place her on a different position along the "interested in work" polarity); "I have the support of the boss more than my colleague" (meaning, I place my colleague on a different position along the "support from boss" polarity); or "My colleague is more interested in advancing his career" (meaning, I place this person on a different position along the "career advancement" polarity). Therefore, according to this model, each time I position another person—each time I create a position-pair—I am doing several things: (1) I am defining myself in the organization along a particular value-based polarity and implying rights, duties, and responsibilities; (2) I am seeing others as "not me" and "not my position"; and (3) I am supporting the values and the culture of the organization by participating in the exercise of positioning. Let us look at each of these in more detail.

1. *Defining myself in the organization.*   Our culture, our community, and our organizations are all sources of meaning for our lives. They provide social environments in which we can interact with other people and, through the use of language, create meanings that we rely on to decide how to act. When we talk to another person, we try out certain words and phrases to see whether our partner will understand them, accept what we are saying, and thereby join us in the process of meaning-making between two people. Gergen (1994) once used the metaphor of

the handshake to make the point that extending one's hand may be done with an individual's intention, but it does not acquire a meaning until it is joined by another hand, at which moment it takes on the meaning of a handshake. The same is true for language: we offer ourselves to others in words, and we wait to see whether our words are understood to confirm the meaning in our own behaviour. And thus the culture, community, and organization are places where we interact in particular ways, with particular values and goals, to make meaning together.

To the extent that we are free agents in our own organization, we may say something that is a statement within a value system, or do something that is an act within a range of understandable actions. We do this with an intention to take a stand, to take a position from which we will be observed and judged by others in the social system. It is what the discourse theorists refer to as subject positions (Davies & Harré, 1990). For example, in the organizational context we may be free to challenge a policy we disagree with, and when we take this position, the meaning of that act for the organization will be generated when others begin to respond to us. Some will agree, some will disagree, but when we take a position we make it possible for others in turn to position us. Our behaviour is then attributed meanings such as: "She is the person who disagreed with the policy."

Another important point is that our own culture, or community, or organization offers us only a limited number of possible ways of making meanings (Parker, 1992). There are a limited number of discourses in society, and each culture offers a different, but limited, range of value-based position statements that a person can choose from. For example, observers have noted that in Eastern cultures, there may be discourses and subject positions about cooperation and saving face, whereas Western cultures may have fewer of those discourses and more about achievement and personal fulfilment. Similarly, we step into an organization that has its own culture and its own values represented by the range of value statements a person can choose from in order to take his/her position.

The alternative view is that we have less agency that we think we do. Our behaviour is more a product of being defined by others, or, to stick with this jargon, "we are positioned by others". From the field of child development, we know that a child's personality or view of the world is hugely influenced by the way his/her caregivers give words and labels and thus meanings to the child's utterances. A child is continually "positioned" by the caregivers. So, should the same be true about adult behaviour? Do we choose to see certain work relationships as threatening, or are we led to that view by the way we and our colleagues are positioned by the organization, to see certain things and interpret them in certain ways—that is, the ways that promote the values of the organization? We will leave the reader to ponder this question; however, in our practice we work with organizations as though employees choose their positions *and* are also being positioned at the same time. The side of the coin we choose to emphasize depends on what most helps clients to be able to step back to see themselves as part of this process.

2. *Seeing others as "not me" and "not my position".*   Once we take a position, or become positioned by others, everything around us becomes "something different from ourselves". The philosophical concept of "alterity" proposes that we need "the other" to define ourselves, but while perhaps essential, the differences we perceive can also be a threat to the coherence of our identity. The French philosopher Jacques Derrida (1978), suggested that every word is defined by the "non-word". In the organizational context, this becomes a matter of how the organization manages essential differences and diversity on the one hand, and how it maintains coherent values and practices within the company culture on the other hand. For example, multidisciplinary teams have the potential to devise interventions for clients in which the whole is truly greater than the sum of its parts, but they also have endless opportunities for misunderstanding each other's position when they describe their clients' needs.

"One member of a position-pair may take him/herself to be positioned in a different pattern of rights and duties from the positioning taken for granted by the other" (Harré & Moghaddam, 2004). When the positioning of one person remains unclear to the other, misunderstandings are inevitable because the same act will be interpreted differently depending on which position that person is holding or is seen to be holding by the other. This is an important point for the consultant because it suggests that conflict between people is not necessarily contrived by either party; it is, rather, that an organization's culture, values, and policies make it likely that a person's actions will be interpreted according to what suits another person's own value-based position. "A position not only delimits the speech-acts available to the person so positioned, but it also serves to pre-interpret what that person says or does" (Harré & Moghaddam, 2004).

Taking a position and being positioned will feel like a benign and constructive process as long as it does not lead to a fixed position with the polarity, and as long as it is not associated with negative connotations. When someone is continually seen as the "person who disagrees with policy", other positions become unavailable and the individual loses the opportunity to change and develop and, of course, the organization loses the new perspectives and new energy that come from being able to shift positions. So, from our perspective as consultants who are called in to solve problems and help people work together better, we see individuals who feel stuck in certain positions within the discourses of the organization.

An example is a large hospital with a surgery department split between two sites. One of us was asked to consult to a process of bringing the two departments together under one roof. A possible way of describing what was going on was that within the profession there were important discourses that were about developing surgery and building strong services that could compete for resources with any other service; this discourse offered many positions, which were taken by the different staff members. At the same time, there were discourses about the best service for the local patients, which involved one central location. The consultant's job was to explain that there were many possible positions to take within the discourse and that the hospital needed to have each position represented in order to have the debate and enact the diversity that would be necessary to make the best-informed decision and the

> ensure everyone stayed "on board" with the final decision. Decisions taken without some representation of the range of positions operating to shore up the discourse tend not to stick.

Feelings and emotions

How do we account for what people feel in the organizational setting, and can feelings be harnessed to help the process of reaching dialogue and initiating change? Managers and consultants will be familiar with such statements as "I feel energized by our new strategy", or its opposite, "I feel tired and unmotivated when I come in to work". There is also the range of direct expression of feeling among colleagues, such as "I'm really angry about what you said", or "You have let me down by your recent behaviour".

Our model challenges the view that feelings are an internalized state, and it proposes that they result from the positions we take and the positions we are put in by others. Our approach is similar to the work of White (1991), who externalizes his clients' feelings to help them take a broader perspective on what it may mean to "be visited" by such feelings, and also to that of Fredman (2004), who emphasizes how we "do emotions" in relation to certain important relationships, although we take a slightly different view. We believe that every polarity has a range of emotions that are attached to each position. For example:

Emotion: I feel strong   I feel weak

Position: I am a winner   I am a loser

We assume that there is a reciprocal process at work such that our feelings lead us to say and do certain things in the organization which are the equivalent of taking a position (or being positioned by other), and in that position we continue to have the feelings associated with it and are encouraged to have those feelings by the responses of others. Feelings and emotions are expressed within the position statement, and we do not separate them from the position.

Therefore, we will acknowledge the feelings that people have but we do not try to change them. People are allowed to express their feelings as they are. If people do not want to leave their feelings, to us they are representing something important within a semantic polarity in the organization, such as fears of change and difference. We are more interested in changing positions than feelings because we believe that the feelings will follow. If an employee say, "I am very uncomfortable in this team", we would be likely to say: "What is at the other end of this position?" "What is a comfortable position in this team?" And eventually: "What does the connection between these two positions feel like to you?" We hold the view (or take the position!) that the meaning of feelings and emotions can only be created by two positions.

The important positions that people take in organizations are always connected to emotions; therefore, as consultants, we try to listen carefully to client's feelings and emotions as these will lead us to the real problems that may lie beneath the words.

Choosing the best discourse

We have found that discourses can be arranged in a hierarchy, from the general to the specific. Our work may begin with more general organizational discourses, such as those concerning success, communication, competitiveness, or authority that exist in any organization. When people identify their positions, they may not be able to see or appreciate their connection to opposite positions; because there are so many different positions available, it is hard to see how two of them might directly influence each other. So we suggest more specific discourses that touch directly on the difficult feelings or dilemmas that people really want to address.

Using the example above might lead us to move from a discourse of "communication in the organization" to something more specific such as "what should happen when employees are uncomfortable" and from that to a more specific discourse such as, "managing personal conflicts between employees". Finally at this level we may ask people to make a position statement within the discourse such as: "I was really hurt by the criticism Mary made about my work." This statement allows us to make a semantic polarity between "hurt by Mary" at one pole and "not hurt by Mary" at the other. Now we can explore the meaning of their relationship and what is hurtful and what is not and how these two positions are connected. And as we follow the process of moving from the general to the specific, clients report that the process goes deeper into their feelings.

Dialogue

Finally, the purpose of locating individuals on positions within the discourses is to give these people a base from which to begin a dialogue. The position identifies them as belonging to and doing something for the larger organization, but it also identifies them as individuals, free to choose their own positions yet constrained to be positioned by others. There are many perspectives, or subject positions, from which one person can begin to speak to another. Many of the ideas that underpin this final phase of our work are related to Dialogue theory (Bakhtin, 1981; Campbell, 2000; Hermans & Kempen, 1993; McNamee & Gergen, 1992; Sampson, 1993; Shotter, 1993; Shotter & Cunliffe, 2003; Shotter & Katz, 1999).

Dialogue is a form of conversation in which two participants attempt to acknowledge the differences and the "otherness" between them. The philosopher Martin Buber (1970) is one of many who have written about dialogue, and according to him, "Genuine conversation, and therefore every actual fulfilment of relation between men (/women), means acceptance of otherness." Deetz (1995) connects the self and others in the following passage: "we must go forward to the selves hidden in each moment of opportunity and realise that the irreducible conflicts between our many legitimate selves are not different from the conflict with diverse others" (p. 223).

Using the Semantic Polarities model, we enable people to identify different positions. These may be different positions that one person takes in different contexts, or it may the different positions available to people within the same organization. But the important point is that dialogic process only occurs between two positions, each recognized as "other" to the other.

Each position implies rights and responsibilities, and, in the context of participating in dialogue, we would argue that we all have responsibility for making a dialogic conversation happen. We have a responsibility to be interested in what the other is saying; we have a responsibility to be influenced by the conversation; and we have a responsibility to speak to another in such a way that they can disagree and add their own contributions.

Penman (1992) proposes four criteria that can be used to describe a dialogic conversation:

1. the talk is responsive to the social realities of the moment ("constitutiveness");

2. the talk must be open to constant revision ("contextualness");

3. the talk must recognize the right of the other's views to exist and to be taken seriously ("diversity");

4. neither the communication nor the meanings created through conversation can ever be complete ("incompleteness"), nor can they arrive at certain reality. "Certitude walks hand in hand with the eradication of the other" (McNamee & Gergen, 1999, p. 20).

There is also the question of what motivates two people or a group to engage in dialogic conversation in the first place. How does a consultant or manager summon the motivation for this undertaking? From within the dialogic framework, we try to interest our clients in the idea that our positions, and therefore our sense of who we are in the organization, depends on the way we are defined and positioned by others. Therefore, if we aim to shift our position—that is, if we want to think and feel differently and to move from a stuck position—we can only do this by taking some responsibility to shift "the other", who then has a new position from which to give us a new position. And all of this shifting of positions occurs through dialogic conversations.

Also, motivation comes from the hope for a better future and from inspiration. The Appreciative Inquiry model that we have discussed is very appropriate for this purpose. By acknowledging what is going well, a consultant connects with that part of the client that has a positive experience, and this promotes motivation to have more of these experiences and perhaps to take a chance on a new, dialogic conversation. Riikonen (1999) asserts: "We could say that problems are areas of experience that are outside dialogue. . . . All interaction and talk becomes a source of social vitality, connectedness and inspiration. What this means is that we are constantly looking for topics and subjects that can be shared and that feel promising" (pp. 147–148).

Clustered positions in the organization

McNamee (1992) introduced the notion of boundaries between centre and margin. The concept of a centre requires the concept of a margin that is populated by the "other". She goes on to say that a person in crisis is someone whose identity as part of the centre is threatened: "A crisis is defined, by its very nature, as a border experience—one on the margin of acceptable performance. A crisis could be seen as a decentralized identity, and as such is thought to open only two possibilities: 1) finding a route back to the centre, or 2) moving beyond the border to another domain, which includes both 'healthier' non-crisis identities and the possibility of the 'abnormal' domain" (p. 188).

The median position

The organization offers a range of positions within the semantic polarity, from the two extreme ends to the positions clustering near the middle, and the differences between the ends and the middle are very significant to how the organization functions.

Ugazio (1998) has described this process in the following way: those people on the extremes define themselves in relation to "the other" and acquire more and more specificity as individuals—"there can be no I without a you". The individual's attention is directed towards the positions of others, and he or she acquires a stronger and stronger sense of his or her own individualism, or what Bateson (1936) called *excellence.*

Those people who occupy positions near the median generate the opposite process, called *centralization.* They are more concerned to maintain equilibrium between the two extremes. Their attention is primarily directed at their own balanced positions, and they acquire less individual specificity or excellence.

When this process is applied to an organizational polarity such as strength/weakness, certain individuals will master the means of being strong while others master the means of becoming weak. The individual develops an excellence, but in organizational terms every excellence is accompanied by a corresponding deficiency. And this individual runs the risk of overspecialization and the inability to respond to changing environments. "Hyperspecialisation in one conversational context renders the individual unprepared to participate in others" (Bateson, 1936, p. 37).

These ideas are helpful for understanding how organizational process becomes polarized; however, our positioning model is not a model of mediation. Our purpose in identifying positions on semantic polarities is to enable people to see the relationship between their position and others around them and then to be able to move to another position. This model can be mistaken for a model of mediation in which a mediator seeks compromise, or a median position, between two polar opposites, but our aims are different. We are seeking to help people take new positions not necessarily "between" two other positions, by identifying their own position and its relationship to others around them; from the new position there will hopefully be a greater potential for dialogue that, in turn, creates new positions within the organizational discourse.

The following is a schematic summary of the concepts we use for our model:

Organizational culture
   is expressed through

Discourses
   which consist of many

Semantic polarities
   which enable people to

Take (or be given) particular positions
   which are connected to

Emotion
   and which specify

Relationships
   and the possibility to create meaning through

Dialogue
   and with dialogue the possibility to

Take a new position

The dilemma

The final part of the process is about finding the motivation for people to change positions or to re-position others within the organization. Why shouldn't they just stay where they are? Why should they go through the effort and the risk of taking a new position?

The answer, for us, lies in the ability of the consultant to identify either (1) a problem with the current positions or (2) a vision of a better future that requires new positions. If we take a problem-oriented approach, which may be determined by the way the organization presents itself, we try to construct a specific two-sided dilemma that represents the feeling of unease in the organization. For example, the staff of a small team may experience rivalrous feeling about one of them getting more career advancement. If we felt it would be helpful to describe this as a dilemma, we might say something like: "The team may experience a dilemma that, on the one hand, they want to encourage ambition and career advancement in the staff, but, on the other hand, it can be very painful when one of your members seems to have some advantage over the others and this makes it hard for the team to work together." And we follow the naming of the dilemma by putting it back to the team as an organizational issue—rather than as any one person's blameworthy problem—by saying that it is an issue to be managed, so we might say: "How do you want to manage this in your team?"

There are several principles crucial to the formulation of dilemmas in the workplace:

1. The dilemma should be described as a tension between opposite points of view or actions.

2. It is helpful if the dilemma is phrased as something people aspire to do—that is, something that addresses the values that encourage people to move forward together.

3. This is based on the idea that people do want to move forward, and what may seem like sabotage of the team ethos is seen, in this model, as an incomplete management of the tension between individual and team needs.

4. The dilemma should be specific and should represent the tensions and difficulties that people currently feel within the team.

5. Once named, two things are important: (a) the consultant should metaphorically "step back" or be silent to let the team feel the two sides of the dilemma as equal pressures that have paralysed them, and then (b) the consultant should persuade the team that they can, through a conversational process, arrive at new positions that dissipate the dilemma and offer a clearer view of how to move forward.

6. By asking the team "how they want to manage the dilemma as a team" the consultant is removing the problem from an individual and "normalizing" it as part of the group process that happens in teams and something that is dealt with through management strategies.

The naming of the dilemma seems to summon the energy and motivation to change and move to new positions. This process is akin to Cognitive Dissonance theory in psychology (Festinger, 1957) and Kelly's (1955) Construct theory. The dilemma is uncomfortable, and it triggers one's need to move away from the discomfort by finding some resolution of the two conflicting points of view. In this way, cognitive dissonance, transferred to the team context as "positional dissonance", is the consultant's greatest ally for change.

Committed conversations

In a previous publication (Campbell, 2000), we explained our view that the organization is created through a series of conversations and proposed that organizational change was then a matter of new conversations among appropriate people. However, Ford and Ford (2003) have taken the conversational model one step further by identifying different types of conversations and the specific process that leads to organizational change, and we have found their model helpful in our work.

They make a distinction between uncommitted conversations that are *about* something and committed conversations that are *for* something. In a committed conversation,

> one is willing to be held to account for their speaking, and its effects and impacts. As a listener, the participant is similarly accountable for what is heard or noticed in the conversation. In a committed conversation, both the speaker and listener are engaged in and accountable for moving the action forward. Committed conversations, therefore, are conversations that create, direct, and forward the action and for which the participants are accountable. [p. 147]

The other contribution that these authors make to the advancement of this model is that they have identified four types of committed conversations that broadly follow the sequence of conversations that will lead to organizational change.

1. *Initiative Conversations*. These are the initial statements that something needs to change in the organization,

such as "we must re-structure our budget, in order to meet our targets for the next year". While most of these conversations will fade away, some of them will be explored in the next phase of the process, *Conversations for Understanding*.

2. *Conversations for Understanding.* Here the initiative conversation is explored and tested by discussing in detail the underlying assumptions and the case for change. This helps people be clearer about the position that people in the organization will take in relation to the change. Some will be for it, some against. Ford and Ford make the point that it is important to be aware that these are conversations for understanding, not for action, and although someone may fully understand an organizational change process, it does not mean they can be called upon for the appropriate action that will move things forward.

3. In order to move the organization forward through a change process, *Conversations for Performance* are required. These "call for a commitment to produce specific actions and results in time, not on the transmission of a request or promise and not on their meaning" (Ford & Ford, p. 150).

4. The final stage is *Conversations for Closure*, which acknowledge accomplishments, failures, and what has been and not been done, all of which allows the past to be consigned to the past and creates the possibility for new opportunities.

While this distinction is helpful in creating a conversational model of consulting, we take this model a step further, by placing both committed and uncommitted conversations on the same polarity. We would assume, for example, that the uncommitted conversation is a type of conversation that represents a position within a discourse labelled something like "ways of communicating in the organization" and that each type of conversation is defined to some extent by the existence of the other. In order for an employee to be confident that he or she is having a committed conversation, the employee will have to have some experience of what an uncommitted conversation is like. Within certain discourses, it may be essential that the committed and uncommitted conversations live side-by-side. So, instead of trying to define a committed conversation or asking the question "are we having a committed conversation?" we would be more likely to ask: which are the discourses that need to be identified that allow everyone to have a committed conversation and that draw other distinctions for the organization? For example, a discourse about "prerequisites that make committed conversation possible in this organization", while wordy, would create different positions that could be taken and then debated with colleagues at other positions.

CHAPTER THREE

Putting the model into practice

Over the years that we have been using the Semantic Polarities model with organizations, we have come to apply the ideas in many different ways. This range of applications will be apparent when the reader comes to the case studies, as we have purposely offered many case examples to highlight this aspect of our model. There are a few of our central concepts that can be applied in many different ways. After all, we are two authors, from different cultures, working with many types of organizations and presenting problems in the public and private and voluntary sectors. Nevertheless, many people have asked us to try to describe our work in a systematic way so that others, whether consultants or managers, can use the ideas themselves. We therefore thought it would be helpful to try to generalize and condense the work we do into a rough template that has some order and sequence. The reader might find it beneficial to think of this chapter as a hypothetical template that can be used to organize one's own thinking and practice when using these ideas in real organizations.

When we put our model into practice, we, hypothetically, will be thinking about five steps in sequence. These are:

(1) identifying the ISSUES that are on peoples' minds when they approach a consultant with some problem, then (2) moulding the issues into DILEMMAS of action. In other words, we try to help the clients articulate their dilemma about whether to move in one direction or the other. (3) The dilemmas are specific enough to then identify the VALUES that are associated with the different choices of action, and (4) the values themselves can be polarized between "more or less" or "better or worse", or "developed and undeveloped", and so forth, which allows us to identify the POSITIONS that people take within the value continuum. And finally, (5) NEGOTIATING CHANGE is what enables people to shift themselves and others to new positions and a new view of what is going on in the organization. Let us discuss this process in more detail.

Issues

Identifying issues is really about engaging with the clients and listening carefully to what is on their minds and what they think is important to them and what is going on in their organization. We ask broad questions such as, "What is it like for you to work in this organization?" or "What are the important issues for you working in this organization which you think we should be paying attention to?" We may also ask questions with a less personal focus, such as, "What are the important issues which influence the way this organization is working" or "Are there specific issues or problems we should address in trying to improve the way the organization is functioning?"

And we get a wide range of responses to these questions—here are some frequent ones: (a) "We don't really feel like we are a team"; (b) "There isn't enough respect among our colleagues"; (c) "We need a clearer direction from management"; (d) "There is too much fear of making mistakes"; (e) "Many decisions are made on the basis of personal relationships rather than open discussion of the issues."

Dilemmas

From the client's initial presentation of the issues on his or her mind, we try to reduce the issue into a dilemma of action. We apply the question, "How does this issue translate into a dilemma in which you are not sure whether to act in one way or another?" So, for example, if the initial issue is "we don't really feel like we are a team", we would ask how this issue of "teamness" makes it difficult to know how to act in the organization. Would they, for example, be interested in talking to others about their work but then feel reluctant because they were unsure how supportive others in the team would be? At this stage we certainly appreciate the consultants' joke about the client who approaches a consultancy firm asking if she can hire the services of a one-armed consultant. "Why on earth would you want a one-armed consultant?" asks the firms' director. "Because we have already employed a number of consultants, and they all say, 'on the one hand . . . but on the other hand', so now we are looking for a consultant who only has one hand."

We are happy to risk losing the contract with this client because we find it is very helpful to translate vague ideas or complaints into specific dilemmas that bear on the client's ability to take action; by placing these ideas in a binary, dialectic form, we are introducing the notion of tension between two courses of action. This tension, as discussed above, is a driving force that will fuel the individual's change of thinking and change of behaviour. Just as nature abhors a vacuum, people abhor the feeling of being trapped within a cognitive or behavioural conflict.

Examples of how we might translate the initial issues into dilemmas are:

> a. *Not a team*—employees may wish to develop their own area of work vs. spending more time with colleagues to produce collaborative approaches to work
>
> b. *Lack of respect*—maintaining the high standards of one's own discipline or practice vs. risking encouraging bad practice through a false approval of a colleague's work.

c. *Clearer direction*—deciding how to proceed using one's own initiative vs. risking getting out of touch with the direction of the organization as a whole

d. *Fear of mistakes*—a need to try new ideas/practices in order to improve my practice vs. fear of being criticized if I get it wrong.

e. *Personal relationships*—I don't know what kind of power I have in the workplace because I am not consulted about decisions vs. it is good to know that there are strong personal relationships holding the organization in mind.

These are some of many examples we could use for this part of the consulting process, but the important point is that we negotiate with the clients to frame their issues in this format and we work together until the dilemma feels right, even though feeling right also means feeling uncomfortable.

Values

Once the issues have been construed as two-sided dilemmas, it becomes easier to speculate about the underlying values that support the dilemma. If we only heard one side of the dilemma from the client's point of view, we would be influenced by that perspective and would have a limited view of the value base for that point of view, but a two-sided dilemma argues for and against the client's view and, by doing so, reveals a higher-order value that applies to the organization as a whole and not just one employee. Clarifying dilemmas is a powerful way to communicate to ourselves and clients that individual dilemmas are contained within larger organizational-level values.

Let us revisit the issues that have now been transformed into dilemmas, to propose some underlying values for each dilemma:

a. Not a team = It is important for individuals to have autonomy in the way they work.

b. Lack of respect = A competitive "us and them" atmosphere keeps people on their toes.

c. Clearer direction = Employees need to know what is expected of them.

d. Fear of mistakes = High standards are jeopardized by mistakes.

e. Personal relationships = Greater trust is ensured through personal relationships.

Two things may be apparent at this point. The first is that these values are expressed as though they could be statements about the organization; the second, that they are definite, declarative, and unequivocal. They clearly represent a single point of view or a single position. One can imagine that many shades of grey are possible when these values are being discussed and interpreted by many people in the workplace. What this means for our model is that many different positions can be taken when these value statements are interpreted and enacted in the actions of the employees.

Polarizing and anchoring

The next step is to polarize the values by anchoring them to two ends of the continuum using whichever linguistic form is appropriate to the way the value is constructed—for example, "more or less", "good or bad", "one or many", "sooner or later". Polarizing is the way to anchor the values across the continuum, and it allows a range of different positions to emerge. The positions now give meaning to the individual's behaviour or speech, and the positions also create a relationship between the position identified and all the other possible positions on the continuum. For example, if we take the value statement "It is important for individuals to have autonomy in the way they work", we can anchor that statement with the linguistic structures "a great deal of autonomy is important . . ." at one end and, "very little autonomy is important . . ." at the other. There are then as many possible positions between those two statements as you care to identify. This will be familiar to many readers as similar to the difference questions and scaling techniques introduced into the field by the practitioners of the Milan family therapy approach (Selvini Palazzoli, Boscolo, Cecchin, & Prata, 1980) and solution-focused therapy (de Shazer, 1985), respectively. The difference is that our model is based on Positioning theory, which leads us to consider the effect upon all the other positions of taking a position or being positioned.

Positioning

We then begin the process of asking clients to position themselves on the continuum, by making statements that clarify their own positions. This also makes it possible to locate positions of others in the organization through statements they might make. Once these position statements are made, we can explore the interaction between them by asking questions such as, "How does your position affect John's position?" or, "What do you see Mary doing from her position which reinforces or challenges your position?"

If we stay with the example of the value statement "It is important for individuals to have autonomy in the way they work", it is now possible to conceive of various interacting positions, such as: (a) "I think there is too much autonomy in this organization and no one is accountable"; or (b) "I can only be creative if I feel free to develop my own ideas"; or (c) "I need to have more direction for my work"; or (d) "management seems too controlling to me".

We do several things once we have reached this stage in the process. (1) We help the clients acknowledge that these statements are merely positions on a value-based continuum that is supported by the discourses and the culture of the organization. The available positions are the result of which discourses the organization uses to define itself, and the specific positions that are demonstrated through the statements are the result of individual choice and placement by other colleagues. (2) We help the individuals negotiate new positions that allow them to see themselves, their colleagues, and the organization differently. With that comes the possibility of seeing new solutions, new directions, or new strategies.

Negotiating change

Positioning theory describes the possibilities and constraints, the responsibilities and duties, attached to each position.

Systemic thinking also leads us to anticipate that one position not only defines other positions, but stimulates a pattern of interaction from others which can be seen as a new system cohering around that one position. For example, Anderson, Goolishian, and Winderman (1986) described the emergence of a "problem-determined system" when one person starts the process by taking the position of describing something as a problem. Other people then begin to interact with that problem-defining position—or, using Lynn Hoffman's inimitable metaphor, they stick to the problem like a tar baby.

As the system develops around a position, the person occupying that position has fewer opportunities to move from that position—and this is where we, as consultants, enter the picture. We often conceptualize organizational problems in terms of individuals holding fixed positions from which they cannot move. One thing that happens when a position is described and made explicit is that people see their attachment to the position differently. It no longer seems like a stuck position. Other possibilities come into view, and the discussion of positions gives validity to many different positions. The one position occupied by the client is not necessarily better or worse than another. Positions are framed as valid points of view, all of which make up a meaning continuum that underpins organizational values. That is why we spend a great deal of time elaborating the many position that are available between the two anchored poles of the semantic polarity.

But there is more to our model than this. Organizational problems are frequently presented as conflict between two people or two groups who occupy different positions on the continuum, and in these cases we often help these clients to have a "dialogic conversation" from their respective positions. We have been influenced by a number of ideas in this field. From the field of dialogic communication we emphasize the listening skills required to really hear what another is saying. From the work of the Public Conversations Project in the United States (Becker et al., 1995), we borrow the structure of each person listening for what the other position means to the person they are speaking to. We pose the question, "Why is it important to this person to hold this position?" And from the field of Appreciative Inquiry, we work assiduously to respect positions and see the positive intentions behind each one. (Our model for setting up dialogic conversations is described in a previous book by one of the authors: Campbell, 2000.)

The dialogic conversation—when it works, which it usually does—unlocks people by enabling them to see value in other positions. It no longer seems that their own position is the only place to be, and, by seeing value in other places, it expands the individual's sense of self and the future, as echoed in Shotter's (2004) concept of "withness" in which one person expands his or her view by thinking "with" the experience of the other.

Dialogic conversation may take the individuals-in-conflict into a new median position between the two original positions. It may also allow them to reappraise the responsibilities and duties attached to their position. They may also see the connection between the two positions, which has the effect of raising meaning to a higher, more inclusive level of abstraction, as though they are saying: "If these two opposing positions are actually connected at some higher level of organization, which I am not aware of, then I may see my position as being part of this higher, more inclusive level of meaning for the organization."

When we, as consultants, get to this stage, we begin to feel that we are closing one chapter in our work—not that we have necessarily completed the consultation, but that we have resolved one impasse, raised awareness of positions, and offered opportunities for people to create new meanings through dialogue. This puts the ball into the client's court to define what these interventions have meant to them and how they want to develop the relationship with us as consultants in the future. For example, they may feel they have concluded the work they wanted to do, or they may want to continue looking at the next phase of the positioning process (since it is endless), or they may want to negotiate for a follow-up meeting to review their progress.

CHAPTER FOUR

Filling in the model

In our work with Semantic Polarities and Positioning in organizations, we have found that the simplicity of the ideas underpinning the model can be misleading when we are putting them into practice. Our own development as consultants has been advanced by exploring some of the related issues that are connected to the model. This fuller understanding enables us to apply the model more confidently to a wider range of problems thrown our way, and this chapter is a chance for us to share our current thinking about these issues, bearing in mind that we are continually having new thoughts.

Power and influence

We feel that organizational work will not be effective unless a consultant has some appreciation of the exercise of power within the organization. Organizations, as the name implies, have to organize themselves with particular structures to carry out particular tasks, and this means certain decisions are preferred over others. Organizations have to pull together disparate individuals and take exclusive and limiting decisions. All of this shapes the environment, takes effort, moves people around, and requires power.

Although there are many definitions of power as a general concept, to support the theoretical framework we are building for this model we feel it is important to construct our own definition: power is the ability to maintain a position and for that position to be influential in the way other positions are taken and maintained. What is implied in this definition? As we have established, opinions and possibilities for action are all related to one's position, so we would argue that positions are imbued with power by the organization. In order to be a manager, and have the power and influence over others that is related to that position, one has to have the ability to take that position and the good fortune to have that position—and its duties and responsibilities—acknowledged by others. And in our parlance, we would say one takes a position of power and influence and is also positioned in such a place by others, such as directors and employees in the organization.

As consultants we would be very interested to learn how this exercising of power works in any particular organization. Power and influence are the lubricants that ease some of the tension between the needs of the individual and loyalty to the needs of the group. Power can be seen as helpful and equitable in this process or it can be seen as biased, narrow, and restrictive. And since the semantic polarity "individual needs vs. loyalty to group" is central to this form of social living, we take it very seriously.

The power of language

We make our positions known to others through action and through the language we use to offer meaning for the action to others. The example that is frequently used in discussions in the media is that one group's "freedom fighter" is another group's "terrorist", and this is very relevant for this discussion as well. The purpose of language in this context is to offer the means, the building blocks, that will allow people from different positions to take the risk of leaving their position and trying out a new position through dialogue with another person. The context for this to happen must be safe, and therefore language has to serve the purpose of contributing to the creation of a safe context, in order to move forward to new positions.

Some words and phrases are so emotive and charged that they make people feel very unsafe, and when this happens they stick to their positions and the beliefs associated with those positions. There are words used in our social discourses that are imbued with powerful connotations, such that when the words are used the connotations follow with them. Words such as "racist", "abusive", "sexist", "incompetent", and the like seem to represent the final word. They have the effect of closing the discussion. They are verbal trump cards after which it is difficult to offer any other point of view, and then people retreat to their own, relatively safe, positions.

But what if people in organizations really feel that they are "being abused" or are the victims of racist behaviour? We would approach this in several ways. (1) We would acknowledge the validity of the statement and the powerful feelings associated with such a statement, and it may be that the emotional tone is so strong that we have to stay at that level and work towards a fuller acknowledgement within the organization of what that person is feeling, since we would speculate that the powerful feelings that have moved someone from a position of professional language to more personal and emotive language is the result of feeling very unsafe about having certain conversations or dialogues. (2) We would, at the appropriate time, make the point that we will, sooner or later, need to think about how people want to move forward and change the way people are positioned within various polarities. We will need to have some new conversations, and to do this people will need to feel safe, and safety, in our experience, is enhanced by moderate, respectful, and work-oriented language.

Does this sound suppressive to the reader? Perhaps you are thinking that this approach will stifle the expression of feelings and miss some of the "real", "deeper", more difficult issues that lie at the heart of the organization's referral in the first place. The answer to this can be found in the way one assesses the organizational issues and what is needed for people to have different conversations together. If one assesses hurt feelings and serious gaps in mutual understanding, these may need to be addressed head on, as it can be very helpful for people to express their feelings and have them heard in a setting in which they do not produce rebounding accusations, which soon leads to mutual blame. On the other hand, the strong feelings can also abate through the experience of beginning to have different conversations in which each participant is able to tolerate a range of different views from the other. Sometimes asking people to suspend their emotive beliefs and feelings for a while in order to reinstate appropriate work-based language allows things to calm down so that each can listen to the other in a different way.

Positions A, B, and C

We use a simple formulation to talk to clients about levels of meaning in organizations. It is based on the Semantic Polarities model but uses different language, which some people prefer as a way of understanding higher levels of meaning. We call one end of the polarity "Position A", and the position at the other end of the polarity becomes labelled Position B; we now have our polarized relationship that connects Positions A and B. Then we name Position C as a higher-level context. It is "higher" in the sense that it represents a different discourse from the one that supports Positions A and B, and it contains some aspects of both Positions A and B within it. Position C represents a higher conceptual level of meaning than A or B. It is also higher in a metaphorical sense. We sometimes talk about Position C as if it were an elevated platform from which an observer can look down and see the pattern of relationship between Positions A and B. (We also may refer to Positions A, B, and C as Contexts A, B, and C, rather than positions, because a context is a broader concept than the position as it implies that there are many things that contribute to the construction of a context. This also can make it easier to talk to clients about all the experiences, thoughts, and feelings that lie behind a particular position and give it its poignancy and power. Consequently, the reader will find both terms used in the book.)

Two things have proved important to us with this formulation. First, we can say people "are moved" up into Position C when their original position, A or B, is influenced by the interaction with the opposite position. So, far example, when one person enters into dialogue with another, he or she has the possibility of including ideas from the other position in a new perspective of his or her own. The new perspective cannot be Position A or B because things have shifted, so we call it Position C.

Second, we find that once people have grasp of the concept, Position C can represent a position that is "above" or "outside" the symmetrical, paralyzing conflicts that can arise between people holding Positions A and B. Position C is like an observer's tower and is also like a refuge, a bit removed from the heat of battle. Within this metaphor, we talk about how individuals can deliberately place themselves in Position C to gain a new perspective.

We have used this device many times to help individuals locked in conflict, and, as is demonstrated in a case study below, we have used it with managers who are trying to manage differences among their staff. There are times when managers want to enter the fray within the discourse supporting Positions A and B, arguing, persuading taking decisions, but there are other times they want to be able to step back and observe the process and perhaps invite others to do the same from Position C.

More About Position C

Position C may be illustrated by this figure:

A   B

C

This position often belongs to the consultant or the leader of the process. The importance of this position when solving conflicts has become clear to us in our work. In one case, the fact that the consultant was physically leaning towards one side was enough to make the other side feel that he was not listened to and understood. In another case, the consultant nodded more eagerly to one person's statement than to the other's, which was interpreted as the consultant having chosen sides. It is crucial that both parties feel that Position C is neutral. We do not believe in neutrality in conversations and in being together; we wish only to underline the fact that it is very important that the consultant is aware of the process he is leading. Position C's responsibility for the trust and security that is needed to make change possible is significant.

A case example should help to illustrate the way Position C can be utilized. This case throws light on how Semantic Polarities may be used by managers trying to make staff members aware of their attitudes, without the managers having to be a part of the conflict.

An experienced manager, who had just joined one of our (MG) manager development and consultation groups, had recently moved to another institution. The manager was annoyed that one of her staff members was deliberately avoiding her and being negative towards her. I said that I was surprised that the attitude of one member of staff meant so much to her, as she was such an experienced manager who had brought about great changes in other organizations and had worked with many different people and processes of change. The manager explained that she had not talked to the staff member about it because she did not want a conflict like that so soon after starting. She told us that the member of staff deliberately avoided her and never said good morning to her. I drew out a polarity with the staff member and the manager at either pole. The manager said that this was exactly how she experienced it. It looked like this on the flip chart:

The staff member's position   The manager's position

Wants the staff member
to say good morning   *Does not*
say good morning

I introduced that she might, of course, just go to the person and tell her how she felt about it. But because she said that she didn't want such a conflict at this moment, there was also another possibility: she might use Semantic Polarities, and, when doing so, she ought to change her own position on the polarity line to that of the C-position.

Staff member's position 1   Manager's position   Staff member's position 2

Does not say good morning   *Says good morning*
                        The C position

The manager chose the second option. Her reason was that she could see herself avoiding more conflict than necessary, and she imagined that the use of Semantic Polarities might make the staff member reflect on herself and thus start an appropriate change. The manager thought that she could get more energy from taking this conversation.

After that we talked about how she could construct the dialogue and what she could do to stay in Position C. I asked her how she would get into the C-position. She tried different statements, but felt that she hadn't succeeded. I suggested she ask a question instead. She thought of asking simple questions such as, *Do you sometimes say good morning?* or *What time in the morning do you say good morning?* She could position herself in the C-position. She was looking forward to trying to use Semantic Polarities.

If you want to succeed in using the Semantic Polarities model and tell others how they might use it, it is very important to make it simple. The manager experienced the situation as complex. I tried to talk about it with simplicity. However, it was important to allow the manager to take positions according to her experience and to let her do what she would normally have done. By drawing out a new polarity, I gave the manager a choice. She was able to feel that the solution she chose was her own.

The Semantic Polarities model furthers dialogues and is therefore a useful tool in all processes of change. It is important that the manager appears reliable and authentic so that the tool contributes by supporting dialogue and the possibility of change. It is important that the staff member feels that she is being listened to, which makes it all the more important that the manager uses Semantic Polarities to further the dialogue.

Application of Semantic Polarities model to conflict

In conflicts we position ourselves *against/apart from* each other. Our positions, created by ourselves as well as by the others, will confirm our differences. We use one argument after another to try to convince the other person. In this way both parties will be confirmed in their views that "I do not agree" and "You are not listening to what I say". Let us look at an example that shows how we may feel "forced" to take a position. The work of an executive, a manager, or an employee contains a great number of formal and informal negotiations. If one party begins the conversation by positioning him/herself at the A-position, the other party may find him/herself taking a position further towards the B-position than he or she would normally have done. In this way the first positioning influences the second one, and the two parties position themselves *away from* each other in a way that puts the situation at a deadlock.

These conversations often end in a "lose–lose situation". Both parties lose because the "winner" cannot use the victory, or feel victorious, when the other side doesn't agree or won't play along. The relation between the two is characterized by mistrust, insecurity, uncertainty, and persistent questions like, "Am I being understood by the other side?" Thoughts like this are typical for both parties. A manager who succeeds in this way in convincing the employee, or the colleague who succeeds in winning the discussion, will experience that the "victory" is useless because the other person will not cooperate on a deeper level as their relationship moves forward.

Differences are crucial for this deeper understanding. Organizations need differences, but differences still create experiences of disagreements, opposition, and problems. Often conflicts seem to be based on experienced differences that have been cemented by the mutual positioning that will follow experienced disagreements. In our work in organizations, we appreciate disagreements and the energy connected to them. Organizations need disagreements/differences to be able to develop and to refine their products and services. We use our model of Semantic Polarities—and particularly the concepts of Positions A, B, and C—as a tool to solve conflicts as well as to preserve differences, which are so vital for the further development of the organization.

Conflicts may be seen as a possibility for development. Conflicts are a choice we have, and they offer possibilities for understandings reaching into many areas. When we work with people in organizations, we find that once they begin to think that opposition, problems, and conflicts are the foundation for development, this opens up opportunities to create new and energizing discourses. On the other hand, when differences are experienced as opposition, one positions oneself and the other person in a fixed, "cemented" relationship: you argue and do not listen to the other person's words and thoughts. Arguments demand counter-arguments and thus create their own relation. There is no longer a dialogue going on, but a double monologue—two parallel monologues. The persons involved will move further away from each other.

We have found some of the ideas from Appreciative Inquiry (Cooperrider, 1990) to be helpful in developing this point— namely, the notion that *a problem is a frustrated dream*. By making a continuum with problems at one end and dreams at the other, you create the possibility for movement and remove the inflexibility. When these ideas—that (a) *problems are positions from where there are no possibilities*, and (b) *opposition, problems, and conflicts are the foundation of development and possibilities*—are introduced, people will start to listen carefully to each other, and they will turn to each other and start the process of understanding. It needs to be emphasized that we do not talk about *agreement* here, but about *understanding*. So you might say that problems and conflicts are a shortcut to the understanding that you need to be able to move on.

Our experience is that the model of Semantic Polarities offers the opportunity to move from positioning against each other to positioning towards each other. In practice it means that one does not have to convince the other with his or her arguments, but that both positions start to listen to each other. The mutual listening makes it possible for both parties to move—not agree, but move. In this way, both sides will start to feel responsible for possible solutions to the conflict. We even experience that this kind of work transforms conflicts into development. This has been said many times before among therapists, so why should this method be better than others? Well, that is not the question we ask ourselves. To us the question is how organizations and people may ensure that the energy that lies in their disagreements and controversies is preserved and will be used for progress.

How, then, do we do it? Our method for solving conflicts is to continuously help the parties to see what is good about the other side's position and ideas—but *without* thinking of it as the final truth. The purpose is to create trust and safety on both sides and make each feel that their positions are acceptable and that their ideas are appreciated on both sides and that change is possible. Their minds may open and enable them to see the possibilities in the other person's views and to the possibilities this will open for themselves. The conversation will make each person feel free to see his or her own position, to see that the other person sees that position, and to see the other person's position, and thus it creates license to change rather than builds defences. The conversation creates hope for a constructive future.

Using the model in phases

Working with the Semantic Polarities model in conflict situations has made it very clear to us that success very much depends on splitting up the conversation into different phases. The duration of these phases seem to be significantly important to how the individual person feels to be understood and thus feels able to move—that is, take new positions and position the other person differently. The C-position is responsible for carrying through the different phases.

Phase 1—*each person separately.* A continuum is made with the two persons' statements at either end. Each party is given the possibility to express his or her thoughts and experiences. When working with solving conflicts it is of crucial importance to allow both parties to talk about their position.

The holder of Position C may easily walk into a trap and be engaged in the statements and experiences of one of the two parties. To help avoid this, the holder should let the two parties talk for a very long time in this first phase. And as a result the parties will duplicate the situations and words that they have already repeatedly expressed, both separately and when being together. In this way the situation will become even more cemented. On the other hand, if Phase 1 is carried through too quickly, the parties will feel that they have not been heard, and so the trust and security necessary for the parties to be able to change positions will not be created.

There does not seem to be a correct duration for this phase, but when both sides have expressed their views and thoughts about the situation, the time is right. It is important that the consultant pays full attention to both parties, while at the same time focusing on the process—not on the result.

Phase 2—*crossing over.* It is crucial that the consultant supports both parties in saying something positive about the other side's statements and insists on them doing so. Again, the consultant must be sure to be fair to both parties and, again, be focusing on the process and not getting preoccupied with the result.

Phase 3—*changing positions.* The consultant's task here is merely to ask the parties where they will now position themselves, and which meaning their new position has to them and to their relation.

Phase 4—*new discourses* that may now be constructive/stimulating/challenging to talk about.

Questions for each phase

Phase 1: "Each person separately"
  What are you thinking?
  What do you think is positive/important about your understanding/statements?

Phase 2: "Crossing over"
  What do you think is positive/important about the other person's statements?

Phase 3: "Changing positions"
  Where does each of you position yourself now?
  What do the new positions mean to you/to the other person?

Phase 4: "New discourses"
  What would be good for you to talk about now?

Visibility

In our work with Semantic Polarities, the use of a flip chart has proved to be very constructive. A flip chart makes the process visible and brings the solving of the conflict into focus. This creates clarity to the fact that you have been listened to and shows that are you interested in the other person's ideas. It makes the process simple and easy.

Some of our clients have expressed their experiences with this work by calling Semantic Polarities "Visualizing dialogues".

Using a future orientation

Once we have succeeded in achieving safe, dialogic conversations between people in different positions, it is easier for them to imagine how they can change their positions in the future. We use the same discourses and polarities we have used in a conversation about the present, but simply ask them to talk about how each wants to position himself/herself on that polarity in the future. These are "future conversations". We talk about what each participant wishes to do. These conversations bring about a clearer consciousness about the actual implications of the desired behaviour. They also offer a clear picture of the desired future behaviour in the organization as a whole.

An example:

During a consultation I (MG) was working with people in an organization who felt it a problem that they were not good at saying things out loud directly to each other. It often made them misinterpret each other and talk behind each others' backs. It felt inappropriate in relation to their wish for more clarity and transparency in the organization. A polarity was drawn with *saying things directly* at one end and *keeping things to oneself* at the other. Each person placed him/herself on the polarity, as below. When we put the two polarities, for the present and for the future, one right below the other, it makes visual the possibility of change.

We talked about the first statement as a wish and a necessity for the organization, and the other statement as an expression of care and a wish for not hurting each other:

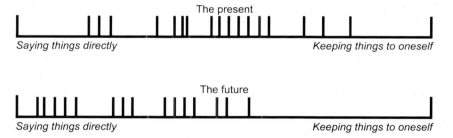

The present

Saying things directly   *Keeping things to oneself*

The future

Saying things directly   *Keeping things to oneself*

After having worked with these two polarities, all the staff members and managers were charged with the task of starting to play with their newly desired positions, individually and in common. They were told to allow mistakes and to forgive each other when things were not working perfectly, and also to notice when somebody succeeded in being in the desirable positions.

If the starting point in a consultation is a conflict, a dilemma between two persons or in the organization, the participants will experience a pressure to change or develop. This pressure often makes people explain why the change has not already been made. "We have not been able to do it, because . . ." or "I have felt that the others have not been aware of . . ." or "The managers have not . . .". These statements are rooted in the past, and they place others in positions that are attached to feelings of guilt and shame. These feelings make people protect themselves against others who have positioned them with these uncomfortable feelings.

Using the future orientation, we create conversations of hope and future (desirable) behaviour for each person and the organization. The conversations explain and emphasize the common interplay, and each person learns a lot about his or her own and the others' positions and thoughts behind the choices of positions. The interaction involves each person's hopes for development as well as the development of the organization.

How to choose a polarity

As in the previous discussion (chapter 3) we have found that it is crucial to be able to choose the "best" polarity. There will be many polarities in one discourse, and once you have found the discourse, you have to work to find the polarity that unites people and interests them in having a conversation.

Once a general discourse is identified, we then try to create a polarity that allows people to take a specific subject position and from which they can make subject statements that are necessary to create dialogue.

We have found that several things are important in choosing a polarity that enables people to contemplate a dialogue with another. Some polarities are better than others, not because they accurately reflect any reality but because they provide a platform for a good dialogue. It is important that polarities are not negative. If either anchoring point is seen as negative, there will be less incentive to listen to someone at the negative end or to risk shifting one's own position towards that end point.

For example, if people were to begin naming a polarity in an organization in which some employees are seen as number-crunching bureaucrats whereas others are seen as creative visionaries, either group could easily negatively connote the other by placing "them" at the negative end of the polarity. It is better for a consultant or manager to describe the polarity in such a way that neither end is negative. So in this case, a polarity such as the following would be less negative and more likely to invite people into dialogue:

| |

Proposes new ideas   Maintains existing structures

But what if people are feeling very negative and angry about the others in the organization? Here we distinguish between the personal level, in which the angry feelings are real and valid, and the organizational level, in which the anger is a position that has a relationship, presumably, within positions; "non-anger" or "extreme frustration" could be matched with a position called "lack of frustration" which invites a dialogue from two positions in the organization. But our model tries acknowledge the personal level—the personal feelings—and then, when the time is right, invites the angry person to consider an organizational perspective in which some people are in positions of frustration/anger and others are not.

Another thing to consider when choosing a polarity is that it must be relevant to the problem or issue on people's minds. They must feel that the polarity accurately acknowledges their current preoccupation and the position it puts them in. We use the term "accurately" because some polarities will feel more accurate or more "right" than others.

Over time, it becomes easier to choose a polarity that feels right, but the best measure of this is to ask the clients—"Does this feel right to you?" or "Does this polarity seem to offer you positions like the one you are in?"

The polarity must enable people to talk and listen. That is the whole purpose. This means we do not judge the "goodness" of a polarity by its ability to "name the truth" or "call a spade a spade" but by its ability to allow people to have a different conversation, and, through this conversation, they will create a "truth" that is right for them at that moment in that context. So, once again, safety is important in choosing the polarity. There is no point in choosing a polarity if people cannot discuss it. If we as consultants feel that some polarities are unsafe or we cannot yet be trusted to sustain a safe environment, we search for a different polarity, one that addresses some aspects of safety in the organization, such as:

| I don't feel fully safe   I feel fully safe

OR

| Some things should not be discussed   Anything can be discussed

Who defines the polarity?

The semantic polarity is defined by someone who has an interest in the connection between two or more points on the polarity. In other words, it is the act of an observer who identifies two positions or who conceives the importance of two positions, which creates a polarity. This could be someone *within an organization*, such as a GP, who wants to refer patients to another service. By being interested in a connection with another service, such as mental health services, the GP places his or her practice on a continuum with the mental health services. A semantic polarity such as "holistic treatment for a patient" is implicit; anchor points for this polarity can be identified such as attention to mental health vs. attention to physical health, and different positions can be identified within the polarity.

Polarities are also identified by observers *outside the immediate organization*. One of us (DC) has been consulting recently with hospital departments that have evolved in different hospitals within the same geographic area. As is often the case with large organizations, there is some duplication of work, and, for reasons of efficiency, management has decided that two services should be combined into one. Here, the managers are placing two departments within the same semantic polarity: "efficient patient care within one geographical area". Although each service defines efficient care differently depending on its history, its personnel and its patient demographic, management now require that they become "bedfellows" in the same polarity. They will need to think about their own service in relation to "the other". Their service will be defined and observed in relation to the other, and eventually the service will have to combine with the other in some ways to create a new position of efficiency in patient care.

CHAPTER FIVE

Case studies with a primary focus on management

We want to emphasize that the Semantic Polarities model is a loose collection of ideas and techniques rather than a prescribed method. This means that we have applied different aspects of the model in the various consultations we have done over the past few years. For example, a conversation about positioning with a staff group may have been sufficient in one piece of work, whereas a more elaborate presentation of Semantic Polarities with flip-chart diagrams may have been necessary in another. Therefore, for this chapter we have looked back over our work to draw out the important interventions and lessons that have emerged from each consultation.

The case examples are based on the recent work that we have done independently of each other in our own working contexts: largely teams and small organizations in the public services in Britain for David (DC), and Danish public and private organizations in social and educational settings for Marianne (MG). The reader may also gain something from reading between the lines about these different cultural settings. We hope the case studies will help the reader understand the model in greater depth and also appreciate the many ways it can be modified and applied to fit particular organizations. Each case study stands alone and was chosen for the book because we think it illustrates a particular aspect of our model.

For us, the "proof of the pudding" lies in the way we have used the model in our work, and the best way for us to convey the range of uses for the model is to present sixteen diverse examples of work we have done in various organizations. For any organization to function well, individuals must be able to collaborate across different roles. One of the most important distinctions is between those who "do the work of the organization" (staff) and those with greater responsibility for holding the organization together as a whole (the management). Our work as consultants can be seen as entering the organization from the manager's position and moving towards integration with staff or coming into the organization from staff positions, where we explore the way staff groups function in order to improve the management process at the other end of the polarity.

So, as a way of organizing the sixteen case studies, we have divided them between two chapters: the first, this chapter, presents cases that begin with management problems and move out from there; the second, chapter 6, starts with staff and team-based issues and then looks at implications for management. Each case is briefly introduced and followed by comments from the consultant who did the work. We have also given each case a brief title extending into the margin to help readers who want to refer back to the cases.

CASE 1
Seeing ourselves as others see us

This case demonstrates the value of understanding how one is positioned by others. Here, the open discussion of positioning enabled the staff to be more participative in managing the process of the team working together.

A psychology service consisting of the manager plus thirteen staff contacted me (DC) to provide consultation to the service, which would involve several meetings. The manager, whom I shall call William, prepared me for the consultation over the telephone. He said the team were complaining that there was poor communication among them because some members felt inhibited about contributing to discussions in the team meetings. Some felt that there was a "judgemental tone" in the group, and some found it hard to say things in front of William. I arranged to spend a day with the whole group and began by asking them to share what they each thought were the important issues influencing the way people communicated in the team, for better or worse. From listening to all their contributions, I began to form a picture of a group of individuals who were unsure of themselves—unsure of exactly what their role was, unsure of how others perceived them, and unsure of how their behaviour in group meetings would be judged.

They also spoke at length about the pressure of work in their service, saying that this made it difficult to protect the space to speak together about their work and the ideas and values that were important in underpinning what they did on a daily basis. They felt they didn't know each other very well, which made it hard to trust others and share their work experiences. This led me to wonder about the organization's discourse about how they were supposed to carry out their daily work, and I invited them to discuss how they thought the team managed the balance between action and reflection. This stimulated a discussion about William's style of management. The group felt that the decisions that were taken by William did not emerge from a thorough, collaborative discussion. This helped me identify a specific semantic polarity based on our recent discussion: decision-making/discussion. I identified these areas of activity as large domains or contexts in which certain behaviours were attributed meanings; these were placed on a continuum to the extent that they were both important contexts for the management of a working team, and a staff member could take a position near one end of the spectrum or the other. In order to put an important boundary around these activities, I labelled them Context A and Context B, so the diagram looked like this:

Context A   Context B

|_____|

Decision-making   Discussion

I then asked the group to position themselves on the polarity in terms of where they are most comfortable in the team, and then I asked them all to position William. The result was fascinating and certainly unexpected. While the staff group positioned William at the "decision-making" end of the polarity, he positioned himself near the end of the "discussion" polarity. This revelation opened up a discussion that helped all of us appreciate that William did not perceive himself as others perceived him. He said, candidly, that his own parents were very dominant and he always strove to develop a collegial style as a manager. He did not want to be seen as a dominant manager or to be authoritarian in his decision-making, so he tended to take decisions behind closed doors. He was struggling to develop a management style in which he could bring everybody on board with the decisions that had to be made. He said he felt more comfortable developing a collegial style that placed him in Context B. There he could be fair and facilitative to the staff group. So it was a revelation for William, and the staff group, to hear that the effect of his gravitating towards the Discussion end and not taking the whole group with him into the Decision-making context was that the group felt that team discussions were not really connected to his management decisions and that the decisions themselves were taken without sufficient collaboration with the team.

This process of consultation got the group very interested in Contexts A and B and the connection between them. I made the point that it was crucial that the two contexts were seen as distinct areas of activity, yet joined on a continuum that enabled the organization to function effectively. What the discussion had done for the group, I suggested, was raise their awareness of the fact that they would need to move back and forth between the contexts *together*, rather than William being in one place and the group in another. The group decided the best way to do this was to empower everyone to become observers of this movement between contexts so that the responsibility did not rest with William or with one or two others with particular vested interests. Anyone in the team could ask: "Which context are we operating in right now?" and, "Are we ready to move from one to another?" And that is where this piece of work ended.

As a coda, I met one of the staff a few months later, and she said the work had been helpful and the team were still asking questions about whether they were in Context A or Context B during their team meetings.

Comment

This case demonstrates that clustering a range of positions into a larger context can be a very accessible idea and a powerful intervention into organizational process. This was particularly helpful in this case because, by reducing the many positions into two encompassing positions or contexts, it mirrored the gap that had opened up between William and his staff. This meant the consultation could focus clearly on how these two contexts represented by William (the manager) vs. the staff (the managed) could come together as one. The other interesting feature of this case is the disclosure made by William about his own background and how this impinged on his management style. This was enormously helpful in this case because the staff could see William as an ordinary bloke trying to manage under the influence of his own values, and they would blame themselves a little less for what was happening. Also, a manager is a huge influence on the way values are articulated within the culture of an organization, and this discussion would allow others to take some risks and bring their own personal feelings into the workplace.

CASE 2
Making room for other positions

This case illustrates that when we stick to our opinion, to one position, others cannot take the same position. So when we stick to our own opinion, we tie up the people surrounding us. However, a renewed dialogue can be started if we set up a polarity. The problem will be visualized, and a new understanding will emerge that we can change our position on the polarity, which will open the possibilities for others to change as well.

MG had a consultation in a small, fairly new school for twelve children with behavioural difficulties. The head was getting tired of having to take too much responsibility. He could not understand this because he had engaged some very competent and responsible staff members. I pointed out that in an organization everybody takes different positions and positions each other. And if a certain position is taken, it cannot be taken by others. I said that at present the head felt that he was taking all the responsibility, but that we could put up *responsibility* on a polarity and thus visualize many other possible positions upon which all members of staff felt they would position themselves. I followed the discourse about responsibility as it was presented by the head and put these two anchor points for a polarity on the whiteboard: *very much responsibility* and *very little responsibility*.

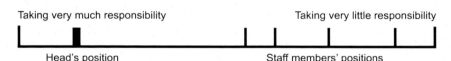

It became obvious to everybody that the head really did take on a lot of the responsibility and that "taking responsibility" was an important discourse that could enable the staff to define themselves as "taking it" or "not taking it". By looking at the polarity, they seemed to understand that there was enough space to differ and that it was possible to take responsibility for well-defined specific areas.

I drew another polarity with the same discourse and asked staff members to position themselves where they would like to be in the future and to give their reasons for the chosen position. I also asked them to specify the responsibility they associated with it. After that, I asked the head to position himself.

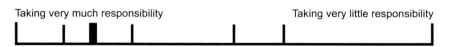

It became clear to the head that he still wanted to take much responsibility—to feel that he had the development of the school in hand. But he also realized that he had to move away from his position in order to leave the staff members room to take it. It became clear that the positions of responsibility had to be in focus permanently if they were to work as a team. There are many forms of responsibility, and all degrees of responsibility should be legitimate.

The head was able to position himself with less responsibility and now saw that the members of staff took their share of it. The head appreciated the staff for taking so much responsibility, which in turn enabled him to make some changes in his management style. The staff appreciated the head for his awareness and his energy in managing the school, the parents, and the staff members themselves.

Comment

Using Semantic Polarities made it possible to change the focus from *reproach* to *possibilities of cooperation*. As the problem was visualized, everybody could be involved in their common goal and was able to contribute in various ways with their different attitudes and abilities.

Using the future orientation made it possible for each of the group to see the possibilities in the changes as well as to see the power of the "new organization". At the same time each person could visualize him/herself in the changes and in the "new organization". And finally each person saw a "plan" for his or her personal changes. Talking about it and seeing their common future on the flip chart together gave them an awareness of one another's changes. At first the different polarities clarified their joint effort; later it clarified their potentials for change.

CASE 3
A polarity for filling a management gap

The following example has been selected from some work with a specialist service (in this case, a psychology service, though the issues are applicable to many services) in which the specialist has been elevated to the position of manager. This can raise numerous issues, such as how the new manager should change his or her relationship with staff and how this person also shifts from supervising specialist work to managing it.

Many people running small specialist services have been elevated to the position from their original roles as specialists themselves. This usually happens as the professional demonstrates a sound competence in the area of work and acquires seniority. The clinician is asked to manage a small team of other clinicians. Because this person understands the task very well, he or she can be very successful in supervising or managing a small group of colleagues. However, as the size of the team increases and the tasks of the team impinge on other parts of the wider network, management becomes more complex.

At this point several things will need to change. The manager will need more time and skills to meet the demands of more complex management, and he or she will need to feel personally comfortable with the new role. For example, management may require more attention to staff development, conflict resolution, and competing for resources within the larger organization. This is not everyone's cup of tea. After all, the elevated manager may have come into the work because he or she liked working as a specialist, and management may now take time away from this pursuit and may seem to require a different set of personal and professional skills.

From the staff members' point of view, we have seen examples in which the staff have great respect for the elevated manager as a clinician and respected colleague. He or she may have been in post for a long time and built up a respected reputation and may well have been responsible for hiring the younger staff members. In small teams, colleagues also develop friendly supportive relationships that span the personal and professional boundaries. All of these things can make it difficult for colleagues to let go of the image of the manager as a respected specialist who has been elevated to management, and to move on to a view of the manager as a manager, which would mean making all the demands of a manager that are appropriate for that role. It also means relating to the manager less as a friendly colleague and more as a person carrying out a role as manager. This is a difficult transition for many a manager and staff member alike. If there is reluctance on either side to make this transition, management can drift without manager or staff realizing what is happening. They say things like "the team lacks cohesion" or "we aren't clear about the direction the team is going" without locating the dilemma within the transitional process moving from a colleague who coordinates a small team to a manager who manages the activities of a large, complex team.

This scenario was illustrated in a consultation by me (DC) to a psychology service that provided specialist input into medical settings. I spoke to the manager, Michael, to get some background to help me organize my thinking. He was managing a clinical staff of twenty and said that when he started out fourteen years ago he ran a single-handed practice, and now it felt like a large business. A few years earlier his stand-alone paediatric service was merged with a psychology department and a department for psychotherapy. I was concerned about how he was making the transition towards a more complex management style, and he seemed to be struggling. There was too much to keep his eye on. He was aware he needed to make more connections among senior management in the larger organization, yet his staff were also saying they wanted to see more of him and wanted clearer directives about what they should be doing. I felt increasingly concerned with how Michael would cope with all this.

The staff team consisted of seventeen junior staff (Grade A) and the manager and two other higher-grade staff (Grade B) who had some responsibilities for managing parts of the service and supervising staff. This led me to develop a line of thinking about the way the three people with management responsibilities (all Grade Bs) were working together and sharing out the burden of the demanding management task. In order to open this theme for the entire group, I decided to draw a polarity on the whiteboard. At one end I wrote Michael's name and at the other end I wrote "Grade As", which left the middle space for the other two Grade Bs who had not been placed.

Grade As   Michael (Grade B)

I told the group I would like to play with the idea that the position of the two Grade Bs was crucial for both ends of the spectrum to feel connected and supported in the work they do, but it is unclear where these two people should be positioned in relation to the others and what jobs they should do from their respective positions. This led to a lively discussion of where each of the twenty wanted to position the Grade Bs, and why. After a sufficient number of justifications were given, it seemed clear to all of us that the Grade Bs would need to increase their level of management activity in specific areas and that this would be a great support for Michael. Following this discussion, I negotiated with the group to come back for a second consultation a few months later to work exclusively with the three Grade Bs to redefine their managements tasks and the ways they wanted to work together.

Management   Distinguishing management
and supervision   from supervision

Another issue that we often see in organizations in which a manager is being elevated from a clinician's to a manager's role is confusion between the need to supervise the staff and the need to manage them. In clinician-based services, good supervision is essential to maintain high professional standards and the high profile of the organization, and since most clinicians are relatively autonomous in respect to their work with their clients or patients, small organizations can tick over very well on the basis of autonomous clinicians being well supervised. It is only when these organizations grow and become more complex—that is, when their work has to be coordinated with other clinicians or other parts of a wider service—that strong, clear management is required. This dilemma lends itself very nicely to the use of Semantic Polarities. For example, within a discourse about "how clinical practice is best maintained in our organization", it may be very helpful to identify the polarity of management at one end and supervision at the other. This exercise allows the whole team to: (1) appreciate the necessity for both positions to be represented, (2) discuss the implications of the different positions, and (3) consider how they can each contribute from their own position on the polarity.

Similar to the situation with Michael, an elevated manager may have begun his or her career as a clinician whose primary mode of achieving good practice was supervision, and the road towards management can be a rocky one. Our experience is that management of larger teams can be rough. There are times the manager has to tell people what to do, to develop a thick skin against criticism, and to wade into conflicts among staff members. It feels very different from doing supervision, and it is inevitable that certain people will feel more comfortable at one end of the "supervision/management" polarity rather than another.

Comment

The Semantic Polarities model is used in a slightly different way in Michael's case. The polarity is structured on the hierarchy of graded posts, from Grade A to Grade B, with space for the other Grade Bs in between, but it is a polarity that supports the discourse about how people should be clustered to provide good management in the organization as a whole. However, as in other cases this also illustrates the use of the Semantic Polarities model to generate a focused discussion. Everyone is invited to take a position and think about the rights and responsibilities attached to each and, of course, to share the exercise as a public event.

CASE 4

Using Semantic Polarities in developing the organization

In Case 4, establishing polarity lines provides the evidence that everybody contributes to the developing process within the framework of the chosen discourses. The various polarities also give the top manager the opportunity to challenge the position of individual staff members. Thus the polarities represent the very essence of the personal development of the individual and the development of the group. At the same time this case reveals the potential of having group development conversations.

MG was hired by the top manager in a large organization. The manager wanted to change both the structure and the culture in the organization by getting the other managers to work together as a group, which they had not done before. The consultant and the top manager had tried in several ways to bring about an understanding of the importance of each individual to the group. This importance finally became very clear through the use of Semantic Polarities. The visibility that was created caused a number of conversations about cooperation among the group. At the same time the managers could see themselves as being a part of the group.

The top manager wanted to generate conversations about development with the entire group of managers. I asked him to state what he thought were the most important discourses in his organization at present. These discourses were set up as semantic polarities and were handed out to the group of managers. As "homework" before the first meeting, each manager was asked to position him/herself on the polarities. The top manager also positioned himself and also had ideas about how he would position all his managers.

In the meeting, eight discourses were drawn on the flip chart, one after the other. Each manager positioned him/herself and expressed his or her thoughts about the other managers' positions, and this led to an understanding that all of the managers were important to the group and to the work of changing and developing the organization. At the same time it became clear that the top manager would be able to move away from his positions if other managers were ready take his positions on the different polarities.

The fact that the top manager had positioned the various managers brought about a dialogue about mutual positioning and led to discussions between the top manager and the individual managers and among all the managers.

Looking at the flip chart together created new understandings. It was obvious to everybody that the group were positioning themselves rather much in a cluster on the polarity, and the conversations made it clear that they all acted as they did without considering what the others were doing. They were just "minding their own business", so to speak.

Here is an example of a polarity (the position of the top manager is indicated by the thicker line):

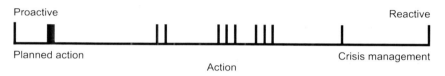

I started each conversation about the polarity by asking the managers—and finally the top manager—to position themselves on each polarity according to where they had positioned themselves on their own homework sheets. After the conversations about what was behind their individual positions, I asked each manager to position him/herself regarding his or her ambitions for development within the next three months. These visions of the future created an image of a more wide-ranging group of managers, respecting differences and understanding one another as contributors. They realized the value of cooperation and of dividing up the roles.

This is the diagram now (with the position of the top manager again emphasized):

At a follow-up meeting one year later, three of the managers in the group were new. In preparation for the meeting, the top manager and the new deputy had chosen two discourses for the conversation, and the group of managers had chosen another two. They had been asked either to choose from last year's discourses or to create new ones and then make the polarities.

First we worked with the polarities chosen by the top manager and the deputy, and then we worked with the polarities
chosen by the group. At each polarity, I asked everyone to position themselves in the present situation and then three months
into the future. After this, I asked the members of the group
what was behind each of their positions and then asked the
group as a whole what thoughts the picture of the polarities
gave them. The conversations among all the managers and the
top manager created both an understanding for each of the
group members and understandings about them as a group.
The dialogue quickly made the managers see how much they
as a group had developed since the year before and how great a
change the new managers had meant to the entire group.

In this way, the new managers quickly became well-known to
the group. We looked at the flip-chart sheets from the previous
year and compared them with the ones we had just made, and
the positive progress the group of managers had made was
obvious.

Comments

All members of a group position themselves and position
each other. Using Semantic Polarities and going through the
process of taking positions makes the positions become clear to
everyone, and one can talk about oneself and each other in a way
that feels respectful to all participants. When Semantic Polarities
are used in groups to address relationships and desires for development, they are a powerful form of team building, because
you both work with the present relationships and make visible
the expectations for development of individuals and the group.
Making everyone's positions visible and having dialogues about
them brings about a strong feeling of responsibility.

This case also shows how important it is that the top manager
is serious and responsible for development and makes sure the
work is written down and filed properly, so that the consultant
is able to use the work from previous years. One is then able to
look at the sheets and actually see the progress that everybody
has been talking about.

Positioning oneself to feel freer to act

In this case, a polarity is drawn out on which the same person is positioned at both ends. The case explains that Semantic Polarities may create a broader space within which a person can work. In this environment, the person will feel free not only to position him/herself at either end, but will feel that there are many possibilities in which to position him/herself, many possibilities to act. In this way, it becomes easier to forgive oneself when one is not doing what seems to be the best thing to do. One's self-perception becomes more differentiated and one may feel free to play more. Focus changes from seeing the things one does as "wrong" to seeing them as "all right" and that there is more than one way of acting.

In a long-term consultation with a manager, MG used Semantic Polarities to help the manager not be too hard on herself. The manager sometimes saw herself as a "taking-too-many-decision" manager. She wanted to be seen as a good "process" manager. In a consultation she put forward this problem: she did not like the picture of herself "overruling" members of staff. I introduced a polarity with *process management* at on end and drew the following line:

Process Management

I asked her what should be put at the other end, and she answered, *"Taking decisions"*. So I wrote it at the other end of the line:

Taking decisions   Process Management

I asked her what was positive about *taking decisions* and *process management*, respectively. In this way the manager was able to see several positive aspects of both positions. We talked about the fact that, as a manager, one is hardly ever stuck in one of the two positions, but that one often moves on a line from one position to the other. The manager started to think of herself in the position of a "taking-decisions" manager as a part of being a manager. She was able to see that it was useful in several situations. We continued to talk about the polarity during the remaining time of the consultation. At the end of the session, the manager stated that she had accepted that she had to do both, and that this was all right. She could now look at herself in all possible positions, and it was a rewarding experience for her in relation to her leadership development.

Two months later, the manager came to another consultation and told me how helpful the previous consultation had been. But now she had met another challenge. She wanted very much to involve her staff in the process of developing their institution. She wanted them all to look at themselves as part of a team.

I said that you can define "team" in several ways. A certain member of staff may look at himself as a part of a team, whereas his colleagues do not see him in this way. I pointed out that the manager might have staff members who would be able to define themselves as team players, in different ways. For example, one way to understand "team" might be as "solidarity"; another understanding might be that our differences are important for forming a team. The manager was able to relate to this explanation. She was inclined to relate "team" to "solidarity".

I drew out another polarity, with *team/solidarity* at one end. The manager chose *team/differences* for the other end. She explained the difference between the two as if she were "leaning back" in the *team/solidarity* and "leaning forward" in *team/differences*.

Team defined by differences   Team defined by solidarity

Leaning forward
(making decisions)   Leaning back
                                                                                    (managing processes)

As the manager saw the polarity, she immediately recognized her previous polarity *making decisions/managing processes,* so I put these statements on the polarity. She realized the connection and was able to add a physical aspect—that she, as manager, would be able to lean forward or lean back. This added a dimension of play to her work with positions of management.

Comments

Semantic polarities make it possible to see that between two poles there may be a lot of possible positions to take up. You are not either/or: you may be both. This knowledge can make your choice of position clearer to you, and you can perform with more clarity in each position.

It is important for us when we set up a polarity in which the same person can take positions at both ends that we allow the person to express that one end is more comfortable than the other. Through the dialogue, we then let the person work his or her way into realizing the usefulness of the opposite position. Therefore, it is important that we allow the person to name the opposite position and that the consultant refrains from drawing attention to the good qualities of this new position, which enables the client to find the good qualities him/herself.

CASE 6
Making a polarity for hidden worries

"We don't communicate" is probably the most frequently heard complaint that working teams present for consultation. But inevitably it is difficult for someone within the team to see a larger pattern of communication; instead, they see one part of the whole and assume that if they are not communicating in a way that suits them, then there is a "communication problem" for the entire team. Our rule of thumb is to begin our exploration by assuming that the individuals are communicating with the people and in the manner they need to communicate. A dictum within the systemic field is: one cannot not communicate. They may not be communicating with the people in the team, nor may they be communicating as expected by others, but they are doing what must be done. This position shifts our thinking towards being curious about who is being communicated to inside or outside the team; what

manner of communication is seen as necessary; and for what other reasons is this important at this time.

This situation was highlighted in a consultation one of us (DC) did for a team of twelve psychologists who worked in schools over a large rural area. The team leader introduced the issues for the team in a long phone conversation, and we agreed to spend one day, an "away-day", with me consulting to the entire team. She described two problems with which the team wanted help: (1) They were about to reorganize their services into multidisciplinary teams in the community, and they would be reapplying for their jobs. They would be less attached to specific schools and were feeling anxious about this major change of role. (2) The members of the team felt they were not communicating well, nor could they raise sensitive issues with the team leader herself.

My first thought was to look for a connection between the two "presenting problems". I asked the team leader what she thought, and she speculated that people were listening to each other less because they were worried about themselves, and they were also contemplating the end of the team as they had known it. We discussed this possibility, and I added that people may be looking for a different type of leadership from her at this time and may be unsure if it was available to them. Perhaps they were looking for a leadership that openly talked about anxieties and anger and provided some security and certainty about an uncertain world.

At the away-day itself, which was attended by the manager and her staff, I decided to put some of these ideas into a discussion about the fact that different people will be dealing with the upcoming changes in different ways and will continue to communicate with others in a way that suits them and their way of managing these anxieties. I drew a semantic polarity on a whiteboard, with "open communication" at one end and protective communication at the other, because I wanted to represent these positions in a positive light rather than accept the group's construction that there were such things as good and bad communication, or open and closed communication, which have a negative connotation.

Open Communication   Protective communication

I also thought many of them might need to find a way to protect themselves, and this process should not be dismissed as poor communication. And, once again, by placing these positions within the polarity, they are reframed by the polarity itself, and it becomes clear that there is a relationship between these two points of view; they exist together and influence each other, and there are many valid positions in between. I then asked them to move into pairs to discuss together what the two poles meant to them and where they would each position themselves and where they would position their partner on the polarity. (I thought afterwards that it may have been more effective to ask people to position "the other" first, as this gives the positioning process a bigger impact.) Following the discussion, I raised the point that being in a time of such uncertainty might lead them all to look for a different style of management, from themselves and from the designated manager.

So, with these thoughts in mind, I suggested to the group that from each of their roles—that is, team members and manager—they were looking for something to help them manage their own individual uncertainties. In other words, they were looking to "the other" for something that made their own situation more bearable or moved them a bit further along the semantic polarity away from uncomfortable positions. This proved to be a popular suggestion. I asked them to go into pairs again to discuss the following polarities in terms of where they would position themselves and colleagues as team members:

Feeling insecure   feeling secure

And where they would each position their manager's priority:

Staff need to be managed   Staff need to manage
by me   themselves

Once the group were thinking in these terms, it became much easier to discuss openly the criticisms that team members had for the leader. Criticisms are bearable—that is, they can be listened to—when they are not seen as personal attacks; the positioning work done beforehand enables people to see their own feelings and behaviours towards the others as an attempt to create new positions.

Comment

This case highlights the importance of using two polarities to demonstrate the role differences between the manager and her staff, yet they are unified because they are all concerned about the same thing: an uncertain future.

CASE 7
Influencing a manager's self-awareness

This case shows that working with Semantic Polarities can change a client's awareness of his or her contribution to a difficult relationship. It is an example of how we work with a primary client, such as a manager, who identifies a difficulty in a relationship with a staff member who is seen as "having a problem". And when this work is effective, both the primary and secondary clients are influenced by the process.

MG has provided long-term consultation to a group of managers from a variety of institutions. At one of the consultation meetings, a manager said she wanted some ideas about how to support a member of her staff who, due to an illness two years earlier, had started working part-time. The manager told me that this member of staff felt:

a.   that she did not have the same work opportunities as before;

b.   that she could not manage to take part in all the activities, due to her illness; and

c.   that she had too much work.

We considered that the staff member may have felt hurt by the changes in her life, which would have affected her self-esteem and self-confidence, and was influenced by resultant negative thoughts that might have a great influence on the way she positioned herself in relation to the tasks and initiatives within the institution. The manager felt the same way. She was beginning to think negatively about the situation. The manager wanted to learn how she might support this member of her staff to have more positive thoughts about her work and her situation in general.

I asked the manager what she had done so far. She told me that she had talked to the member of staff on several occasions and tried to convince her that she was doing fine. The manager had tried to make distinct agreements with her as to what she was supposed to do. On several occasions she had tried to offer her certain tasks, but she had not wanted to take them on.

The manager was running out of ideas and had started to think negatively about the staff member, even though she knew that the staff member was very good at her job.

I suggested that the highest discourse could be *understanding oneself* and that we could identify three polarities within that discourse that were represented by the conversations they had had. Statements from the conversations would all be put at one end. The simplest process then would be to talk about the other end of each of the polarities. The manager agreed and said that perhaps she could use the same process with the staff member. The positions on the polarities looked like this:

Not having the same possibilities
as before

| |

Cannot manage to take part
in all the activities

| |

Having too much work

| |

Normally we do not put up the negative statements, as it is very difficult to initiate a dialogic conversation with someone who is seen in a negative position. These personal statements represent positions. Only the person behind the statements can choose to take new positions. Instead of telling the staff member that she is doing OK, I suggested that we tried to look for the opposite positions in all three polarities. So I asked the manager what she thought her staff member would say were the opposite statements. The manager considered each of the polarities and came up with these:

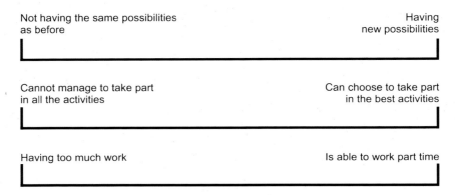

Not having the same possibilities
as before

Having
new possibilities

Cannot manage to take part
in all the activities

Can choose to take part
in the best activities

Having too much work

Is able to work part time

The manager said these discussions made her think that it was not a matter of one way or the other, but that putting up the polarity lines gave her a feeling of being able to choose between several positions. The manager wanted to use the same process with her staff member in order to help her in her struggle.

At the end of the session, the manager felt that she had obtained a new understanding: how to create possibilities to get what we want. She felt that she had obtained an easier approach to talking with the member of staff again, as well as a tool to open the next conversation. We spoke of the importance of creating the same kind of process with the staff member, so that she got the opportunity to experience the same kind of relief and to have the same insight. Six weeks later, in a new consultation, the manager reported back that she had not had the conversation with her staff member. She herself had felt better with the situation since the last consultation. She had not felt the need to talk with her staff member. She also said she did not feel comfortable initiating the conversation and that she needed more consultation from the group about having individual conversations with staff in her own way. (You will hear more about that later, in our next book.)

Comments

This case illustrates that the positions we take and the way we position other people has a big impact on our sense of self. If we can get into the conversations about positions, we open ourselves to the possibility of new thoughts, and that again will influence us in taking and giving new positions.

In consultations as well as in other types of dialogues about ourselves and others, about actions and thoughts or about reflections, our lines of thought may easily get too complicated. We often use the metaphor of crossing the river again and again to fetch drinking water. When we work with Semantic Polarities we can simplify this process by simply talking about the opposite pole. In terms of the metaphor, we call this: walking down to the river to drink the water.

CASE 8
A telephone reminder about Context C

This case shows how an expected conflict is redirected with Semantic Polarities—via a telephone call. The basic condition for this quick change of focus is that both parties are familiar with Semantic Polarities and are able to use them on a daily basis.

A former participant in one of MG's consultation seminars phoned Marianne and said that she needed a change of focus and that she needed it fast! As a manager of a staff group, she was going to enter into a discussion on smoking policy at the next staff meeting at her workplace, which is an institution for multi-disabled children. A group of staff were proposing to use a room in the middle of the building for the smokers among the staff . She anticipated that everybody would expect her to stand up against this proposal, and she expected that some of them had prepared themselves for her opposition. She wanted ideas on how she could use Semantic Polarities to avoid having to argue back and forth with the staff. How could she contribute to the creation of a dialogue on smoking policy that would help the institution make an informed decision?

I started from what she had said about smoking (the discourse) and positioned her statement about *smoking in the building* at one end of a polarity and the simplest opposite statement *smoking outside the building* at the other. Then I suggested that she drew out the real dilemma about smoking: *pleasure for adults* and *health risk for children*. If she were to draw up another discourse labelled *smoking policy* with *children* and *adults* at either ends of a polarity, she might inspire the staff to engage in a dialogue about the two sides of the polarity. Also, she might suggest that the participants should look at both discourses and think about their decision with consideration for both of them. Most importantly, she should see to it that both discourses were drawn out as polarities on the flip chart (visualization). Her position would be to view the process from the position of Context C and, in that position, help her organization to make the best decision.

Comments

When a person is involved in the dialogue and at the same time is managing the process of using Semantic Polarities, visualizing the discourse seems to be crucial. The visual image of the polarity works as an externalization of the process and that makes it possible to change more easily between Position C and Positions A and B on the polarity line. The very thinking of being able to use Semantic Polarities created the idea of a focus shift from being stuck to being unstuck.

CASE 9
One person taking two positions

This case shows how Semantic Polarities may be used by a new manager for getting a positive start. She has a great desire for having a clear, direct, constructive, and open dialogue with staff members from the outset. The manager also has at heart a desire to position herself as a qualified and competent manager.

A manager who had just moved to a day-care centre for children aged from 1 to 6 years wanted to be acquainted with her staff as quickly as possible. I (MG) used to work for her as a consultant in her previous organization. She contacted me and expressed her ideas of making "conversations of expectations", as she called it, with each of her staff members. She wanted the conversations to begin with the same questions being presented to each staff member. She wanted these questions to be simple and to the point and for this process to be completed in two weeks. Through these conversations she wanted to position herself as a qualified, competent, and involving manager. I asked her what she thought about her new organization and which three discourses she found most important in relation to it. She mentioned a positive attitude, the contribution of everyone to the progress of the institution, and how she and her staff could promote development in each other. I asked her what she found important about each discourse, and we agreed on three discourses: *work, change, and leadership.* Together we drew out a polarity for each discourse, along with a few simple questions for staff members as starting point in their talks. She then wrote this in a memo to all her staff members so that they could prepare for the conversation:

I would like to ask you to prepare for the following questions before our conversation. It is important to me to get a good picture of the organization I am so lucky to have become part of. I am looking forward to an open dialogue with you.

Questions:
- *When at work, do you prefer to work alone or together with others?*

- *Regarding changes in the institution, do you wish for few or many changes?*
- *What do you want to do even better in your work?*
- *In which way will you contribute to the positive development of the institution?*
- *In which way do you want the managers to contribute to the positive development of the institution?*
- *Regarding your manager, would you prefer a manager who makes decisions or a manager of processes?*

For each conversation, the manager had prepared a sheet of paper on which the polarities and the questions were lined out. Each member of staff was supposed to position herself on the polarities, which was the simple starting point to a positive dialogue between manager and staff member.

Prefers to work alone   Prefers to work with others

Work

Wants many changes   Wants few changes

Changes

Wants the manager to make decisions   Wants a manager of processes

Leadership

After the conversations, the manager wanted to collect all the papers and report to the staff what she had seen, and then she would invite them all to participate in the dialogue about their common aim during their first year together.

So what happened?

Comments

The experience from this case is that it is possible to create an immediate contact using Semantic Polarities. It quickly gives the manager a clear picture of the organization and brings about open dialogues in a constructive context and within a deliberately chosen framework: the common goal.

In this way, the manager creates a joint focus on the future. Semantic polarities give the new manager both insight and outlook and make her feel able to make the organization move forward—together with staff members.

CHAPTER SIX

Case studies with a primary focus on staff relations

A new polarity for respect

Respect for colleagues is a fundamental condition for good team work, and lack of respect is frequently an unspoken barrier to building working relationships. This case shows that in spite of apparent lack of respect, it is possible to place all members of a staff group on a new polarity that will stimulate a new interest in communicating with each other on a different basis.

We have found that mutual respect—and the lack of it—are at the heart of team relationships. When one colleague feels a lack of respect from others, he or she may retreat from the team and express dissatisfaction by not contributing much to a team effort. This often has the effect of further undermining the respect from others, and a vicious cycle has set in. Our experience is also that when one colleague expresses a lack of respect for another, it is usually the result of people working from different values. If one asks why one person does not respect another, what is usually said are things like he or she is "lazy . . . unreliable . . .

dishonest" or "isn't committed to this job" or "doesn't treat clients the way they should be treated", and so on. Each of these observations can be understood as a discrepancy between the values of the observer, who, for example, values reliability and punctuality, and the colleague being observed who has different values about him/herself in the workplace. One might also say that the observer is identifying two different positions on the semantic polarity of "laziness", "reliability", or "honesty", placing him/herself at the positive end of the polarity and the colleague closer to the negative pole.

In terms of respect, then, we could say the observer has certain values about laziness and hard work, and these values are given meaning through the construction of a semantic polarity and the different positions within it. For example, if I value hard work, my values are given shape and meaning when I can position someone else further from my "hard work" position, in a "lazy" position. In a similar way, my position may become respected, and other positions can be less respected, if those positions are negatively connoted.

As consultants, we have tried to tackle lack of respect by helping a team to talk about the way different positions will be negatively connoted, when it is more appropriate to see other positions as the result of different values that probably have not been spoken about and understood. This means understanding each person's motivation for coming to work every morning—that is, what they bring with them to the workplace—and their motivation for their behaviour once they are at work. Colleagues who are seen as lazy may have personal obstacles, such as illness or family problems, affecting their behaviour; or they may feel de-motivated because of poor pay or advancement possibilities; or they may lack the skills to do the job competently. All of these things can contribute to a value or a belief about coming into work in the morning.

We would say, within our model, that if team members can understand the values inherent in the positions taken and assigned by others, then the team will go some way towards feeling connected with others' values, and thus respect can develop. This makes it possible for a team to have a conversation about the values they want to support in their own team discourses in order to do the work the team wants to do. A team could, for example, move from a discourse such as "everyone works hard in this organization" (which offers positions of "hard work" and "laziness") towards a discourse such as "personal feelings about one's work should be shared in our team" (which offers positions of "more sharing" and "less sharing").

Some of these points were addressed in a recent piece of consultation conducted over a two-month period. An organization providing domiciliary care in the community approached one of us (DC) because they had recently created a new management team to reflect a wider range of operations but the team was not working well together and there seemed to be a clear lack of respect among them. In situations in which a team is not communicating well for any reason, I often find it more helpful to interview the team members individually before meeting them as a team. This has the benefit of allowing me to hear the views of each team member in a setting in which they will be less influenced by the various relationships, good and bad, with the people sitting in the room during a team meeting. I find that in some team meetings, people will be overly polite or overly aggressive depending on which issues are being enacted, and this can make it more difficult to get a clear picture of where each individual positions her/himself in terms of important values. It is also more difficult for people to listen to and absorb another's point of view if they have a point to defend or defeat.

So I set out to do individual interviews with the nine members of the new, expanded management team, and it was quickly clear that difficulties in the team were expressed in terms of lack of respect for the way others were working. What seemed to have happened is that the original organization consisted of a few managers who used a very "hands-on" approach to their work. Their sphere of influence was narrow enough that they knew everything that was going on and could personally intervene to sort out any problems. Their personal approach was effective and was recognized as such by the staff working for them. With the expansion of services, however, these managers could no longer intervene personally and had to trust other staff to sort out problems themselves. At first, the challenges were too much for the new staff and mistakes were made. This was disappointing to the older, experienced managers, and in their disappointment they lost respect for their staff.

I began thinking of the lack of respect as a by-product of this other issue of moving from an organization in which people could be responsible for their work to one in which they were dependent on others with less experience, and when we eventually had an away-day for the nine managers together, I made the point that they would need to suspend their project to respect each other until they had more opportunities to develop new procedures and new working relationships. When they had more experience in this new environment, with more dependence on each other, they could then judge their mutual respect on the basis of how well people managed the new developments, rather than the old values.

We discussed these points, and then I opened up a fuller discussion by posing these semantic polarities for them. Instead of positioning people on this polarity:

| |

People whose work   People whose work
I respect   I do not respect

I suggested it would be more helpful to them to position people on this polarity:

| |

I need to negotiate with   I need to negotiate with
others a great deal   others very little

This was one small piece of my work with the team, but it helped me—and I hope some of them—to see that the lack of respect could be helpfully linked to people working from an uncertain value base.

Comment

Lack of respect was seen in this case to result from a shift of values from independent practice to dependency on others, and the group had no experience of working together in this new way. The new value base could not be established on the basis of experience because there simply wasn't any. The group were judging each other's behaviour on the basis of the old values, and they came up wanting, and this equated with lack of respect.

CASE 11
The messenger position

Two examples are given here in which clients were unable to take one position on a polarity because they felt firmly, and emotionally, attached to many positions. We have called this the "messenger position" because the client is trying to communicate across a range of positions in the organization.

In a residential centre for mentally ill people, the manager and staff members wanted to work on staff development and, specifically, on the cooperation of the staff in working together. I (MG) had worked as a consultant with the organization for two years, so the members of staff knew and appreciated my work.

Starting with the issue of cooperation, I asked them which discourses were important for them to deal with. I then asked them to choose one discourse. Together we drew out various polarities that made sense in relation to the chosen discourses, and then the group chose one polarity:

Doing what I am asked   Doing what I think
to do by management   is good to do

When I asked everyone to position themselves on this polarity, one staff member seemed to feel uncomfortable having to do this. I insisted that everybody had to do so. Her reluctance was growing. She said that she was unable to position herself in one position. I suggested that she position herself in whatever way she thought would show how she was visualizing her position. I said that we might learn more from that than if she held back from expressing her own reluctance in some way. She positioned herself by drawing a long line parallel to and below the existing polarity, like this (the manager's position is emphasized):

Doing
appointed tasks

Doing what one thinks
is good to do

As everybody had positioned themselves when they saw the total picture, it became obvious that the staff member who had positioned herself along the lower polarity line was connecting the two positions further apart. She was holding the role as the intermediary between all the staff, including the manager, especially between the manager and one of the staff members who had positioned herself furthest away from the manager. She said this position was OK for her.

Her position might be seen as an expression of the fact that she was capable of covering a wide range of tasks and qualifications. She felt that this image of her position gave her a lot of space and she could work in the way she wanted.

At the same time, her position might be very strenuous, because she had to connect to all the positions in the organization. During our work on developing their cooperation through Semantic Polarities, she reiterated her positioning and felt that it was the correct position to take, for the time being.

In another case, I was working with a school with all the teachers, the head, and the deputy. We were working with the positions on a polarity between *developing new ideas* at the one end and *implementing existing ideas* at the other end. The head put herself at one end of the line, and the rest of the group positioned themselves on the line, thus:

Developing
new ideas

Implementing
existing ideas

The deputy came to me and said that he was not able to position himself on the line because that would have a negative impact on the group of teachers. He showed me his paper, on which he had drawn a line below the polarity line. I asked him to follow his own instincts about the way he saw his position and just go ahead and position himself. He then went to the flip chart, after the others, and drew the messenger line the full length, but just below, the polarity line.

I then asked everybody to talk about what was behind their position. The head said that she felt it was very important that she was "on top of the development" of the school. The deputy said that he felt the importance of helping all the teachers who needed or wanted to be helped so they could contribute to the development of the school and work with the "old" ideas. It was mostly the new teachers who had positioned themselves at *implementing existing ideas.*

This is the polarity line, with the head's position empha-sized:

Developing
new ideas

Implementing
existing ideas

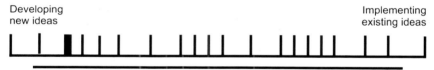

Deputy

By looking at the polarity and all the positions, the head and the deputy could see that they complemented each other. The teachers appreciated both positions. The new teachers, especial-ly, said that they were proud to be in a school where there were a lot of new ideas and where the old ideas were not forgotten.

I said that all the positions were very important because they showed how important everybody was, but I asked them to pay attention to the fact that it can be difficult to be at both ends of the polarity at the same time. I pointed out that it can also be hard to be in the "messenger" position. I explained that one per-son cannot take a position that has already been taken and that in order to be able to take a new position a person has to leave that position. I then asked them to be aware of when someone tried to change position and to try be helpful. And then I would be looking forward to seeing the new picture of the same polar-ity a year from now. They all expressed their energy in trying to change positions in many ways.

Comment

The messenger position in an organization may be illustrated by a creature from Nordic mythology, Ratatosk. Ratatosk is a squirrel whose task it is to connect the top and the bottom of the great tree of life, Ygdrasil, by running up and down, bringing messages to and from the root of the tree, which the snake is gnawing, and the top of the tree, where the eagle is sitting, overlooking the world.

In our work with the Semantic Polarities model, we sometimes find it difficult for a staff member to position him/herself within the chosen polarities. For us, the most importing thing is the conversation that develops out of the polarities, and it may be important to allow the individual members to position themselves on a polarity that they choose for themselves and which they believe more accurately reflects their position. The process is more important than the particular method. When we are dealing with a "Ratatosk", it may be effective to visualize this kind of positioning, realizing that the whole point of creating fruitful discourses is aimed at setting free the "Ratatosk", in the sense that all members of the organization should take responsibility for their own position in the cooperation and development of the organization.

CASE 12
From positions to dialogue

One can see in this case that a cultural value was picked out of the conversation and made into an anchor point for a polarity and became the basis of the beginning of new, dialogic conversations among a staff group.

One of the ways Semantic Polarities can be used is to identify one statement or value that emerges when discussing the culture of the organization and to anchor that statement to one position and then explore the way other positions are taken up by various members of the agency. An example of this comes from one of our consultations (DC) to a small, specialized counselling service which was staffed by six women. We organized two days of work together. At the first meeting they were describing what led them to seek a consultation. They felt they were doing demanding work that drained their emotions, yet they found it difficult to use each other for support. As I listened, one of the staff said, "we are six strong-minded women". This seemed like a powerful belief, which identified an important position within the discourse of the agency. I thought to myself about anchoring a semantic polarity by placing "strong-minded women" on one end. And from that point "vulnerable women" could be the anchor for the other pole. I drew this polarity on a flip chart to create a graphic representation, and I initiated some discussion about how the polarities work—that is, that each position is defined by other positions, and that in this case, they will know their vulnerability in relation to being strong-minded and vice versa. I suggested that it may be difficult to be vulnerable with each other and maintain the belief that they were strong-minded women, which certainly had important meanings within other discourses in their culture such as coping with difficult cases, fighting for agency resources, and being an all-female team. This led to a fuller discussion about what being vulnerable meant to them.

This discussion drifted towards the general, and I thought it would be helpful for them to be very specific about feeling vulnerable within certain relationships, so I organized the second part of this discussion to take place in pairs. I asked them to start by drawing the semantic polarity of "strong-minded women" and "vulnerable women" on a sheet of paper and then indicating their own position on that polarity. From those positions they could begin a discussion about how they would like their partner to understand the way they were trying to manage their vulnerabilities, and how this twosome might make it easier for each to share vulnerabilities about their work.

Towards the end of the consultation, a new theme arose that was also addressed with Semantic Polarities. I asked the group how they used their meeting time, as this is often a crucial opportunity for groups to create new conversations. They described the regular two-weekly meeting, in which they set aside time to talk about their cases. They said they presented cases but felt defensive. As we explored this further, it became clear that they were looking for support for the feelings they carried about the cases but seemed instead to get a range of ideas about how the case should or shouldn't be managed. To me this linked back to the previous discussion about being strong-minded women, and I asked whether they were demonstrating their strength and testing it with each other by offering lots of ideas about managing cases. It seemed as though there was almost a competition to have helpful suggestions for case management.

This seemed to make some sense to them, so I drew another polarity on the flip chart to reflect the differences emerging from our discussion. On one side of the chart was "How I think you should think about the case" and on the other side was "How can I just get into your shoes?" Then, as I usually do, I emphasized that both positions were necessary to manage cases, but there may be uncertainty about what is helpful for a clinician at a particular time. In the ensuing discussion, they refined these positions to the concepts *suggestions* on one side and *connecting with the experience* on the other, and they decided to have a facilitator for these meetings in future who would keep this polarization in mind and raise it with the group at appropriate moments.

Comment

We find this process of polarizing the different aspects of the team activity and holding it in front of people—literally as well as metaphorically— helps them to acknowledge their position and to be aware of the larger context that is leading to miscommunication and hurt feelings. In this example, the two positions "How you should think about the case", and "How I can get into your shoes" are not two opposed polar positions on a continuum, but nevertheless they do represent two different positions, and they elucidate an important value embedded in the organization's discourses about how cases should be discussed. And once the positions are identified, people can begin to negotiate new positions that are informed by the presence of other points of view and other values.

CASE 13

Shifting a working relationship between two colleagues

This case is about how we position ourselves and each other when we are in one relationship. When we change this relationship, we also change our positions, our thoughts, and our behaviour.

In a psychiatric day-centre, MG was working with the whole group of staff. Two staff members were contact persons for the same client. They both felt they were disagreeing on which kind of help the client needed. Furthermore, they had experienced that earlier attempts to speak about their disagreement had not been successful for either of them. The way they positioned themselves and each other had created problems in their tenuous cooperation. They both felt that the other person did not understand the client's needs and both felt the other person showed little interest in cooperation.

I drew a polarity on the flip chart, and it turned out that their statements were not even contradictory—they simply just seemed to be speaking different languages. The two poles seemed to make sense to the two staff members but did not provide an immediate understanding for the other staff:

A's statement   B's statement

I do my job   Our task is to make our clients
in the best possible way   as independent as possible

I started by using the phases from "solving conflicts" (see chapter 4), in which the two sides at first talk about their own thoughts, then about what is positive about the other person's thoughts, then about their new positions, and finally about what at this point they would find helpful to discuss further.

In their conversation about what was good about each other's statements, they started to listen to each other and talk about what they had seen the other person do that was beneficial regarding the client they were both attending to. When they were asked to take a new position, they actually crossed positions on the polarity!

A's statement

B's statement

B2   A2

When I asked B where she now positioned herself and what was behind her new position, she said that this was the first time she had understood the reasons behind A's work with the client. This was the first time she had heard A explaining so clearly why she worked the way she did. And that is why she wanted to show her appreciation by moving her new position so close to A's first position. When A heard that, she felt relieved and happy. She then positioned herself on the other side of B's new position and stated that if B could move that far, she herself wanted to move "a lot" to show B that she was willing to cooperate. And then again, not too far from B because she wanted to be able to talk with B in the future.

I then asked them what had been productive about the process. They said they were both happily surprised by experiencing that the other person had been able to identify so much good stuff about what they had said. They were now able to see that they complemented each other. On previous occasions they had not wanted to talk because they thought that they were very different. Now they were looking forward to talking together and to making use of their differences.

Comments

Several things seemed to help these colleagues have a different conversation. First and foremost, both were willing to express their differences. The visualization of the problem and the fact that they were directed to look at the chart and not at each other was also new to them. To talk about and to visualize the differences without taking sides (i.e. staying in Position C) was a precondition for them to be able to move. Visualizing the positions instead of making the statements "personal" made it easier for them to see each other as a contrast, and therefore created a possibility for a new conversation. The greatest experience for them was perhaps that they were actually listening to each other, which brought about new information and new ideas to both of them. They were both able to change. I thought the use of Semantic Polarities made it possible to allow the two colleagues to work on their own. To visualize their problem on a polarity was an externalization that created the space they needed in order to have new dialogues. They were able to listen to each other and feel that they were being understood, so they no longer experienced the urge to interrupt each other.

CASE 14
A positive use of a negative position

An outspoken negative position became the beginning of a change that no one had ever thought possible.

In a day centre for mentally ill people, the staff wanted some help from the consultant (MG) about their staff meetings. The staff were dissatisfied with their meetings—but for different reasons. Their turn-out was low, and the manager believed that there was too much dissemination of information and too little dialogue.

One male staff member suggested that the meetings should be discontinued. The rest of the staff felt that he was being negative and not interested in the professional development of the group. They regarded the meetings as necessary for their own professional development.

As a consultant I introduced several ideas: (1) everybody's thoughts—even the unpopular thoughts—could be seen as an expression of responsibility for creating good meetings; (2) I regarded criticism as a responsible act when followed by willingness to talk about new possibilities; and (3) the way we look at each other, and at ourselves, was most important. The way we position each other and ourselves has a decisive influence on both ourselves and the other, as well as on the situation in which we find ourselves. Furthermore, the way we position ourselves may maintain the present conflict. (4) I also stated that we can change these positions if we want to.

Everybody was interested in moving forward in the process, so I suggested that we started by listening to the "critic". I interviewed the "negative" staff member from the point of view that he had some ideas about the problem the organization was facing, and I asked his colleagues to listen for what was important and what might create new thoughts. After the interview, I asked all his colleagues to discuss what was good and important about what he had said. Most of them started to say, "I have heard what he said, but I thought . . .". I interrupted these statements immediately and insisted that they only state what was good about what he had said to us. In the beginning, I was helping them by emphasizing that his critique was helping us to be able to talk about the issue, that he was actually expressing his wish to be a part of the group, and that he was interested in sharing his thoughts with them. Then they all started to join in and followed up with suggestions about what else was positive about his remarks. These reflections made the "critical" staff member more attentive. He felt that he was being heard, and he said that he certainly wanted to attend meetings, but with new content in them.

The colleagues were happy to find themselves in a situation where they were having a conversation about an issue that had previously been hard to discuss.

I now introduced the idea that a discourse on a higher level might allow for new dialogues, and we agreed that "staff meetings" would be a good subject of conversation. I pointed out the importance of appreciating differing opinions in conversation and that a polarity could be established on which the different views could be expressed. This conversation, I said, could create a new and better understanding.

The discourse was settled: staff meetings. *Better meetings/ Abandon meetings* were put at either end of the polarity.

Staff Meetings

Better meetings	Abandon meetings

By creating a polarity with these two positions at either end, and by letting both parties express their opinions about what was good about the opposite end, everybody was enabled to take up new positions. A change had occurred that nobody had thought possible: they agreed to go on talking, but now on an entirely new discourse: *good ideas about the content and form of meetings*. They agreed that the various departments should take turns arranging meetings. From that point, the whole organization had better meetings. They reported that the meetings were now full of energy, amusing, and inspiring, and they were discussing substantial issues. The energy of the meetings was shown by the fact that meetings were held in parks, boats on a lake, offices, and many other places. Each agenda was well prepared by the various departments and included everybody's issues. At the same time, all information about the organization was disseminated through their internal computer network.

Comments

In this case, the use of Semantic Polarities created an understanding of the importance of one's own and the other's position and of the fact that we position each other. Thus a dialogue about something substantial was possible. The consultation did not only bring about a change in their meetings; the greatest change occurred in their patterns of dialogue, in their views of each other, in their cooperation, and in their relation to their manager. It helped them move their common task forward.

CASE 15
From old to new discourses

This case is about history and the way it becomes embedded in an organization's culture. By placing new discourses alongside the old, the staff group was able to move forward without discarding their important history in the process.

The director of a long-established psychotherapy organization, whom I (DC) had known as we had worked together on a committee, asked me if I would provide some consultation to the staff team of 16, some of whom were saying they didn't feel well enough connected to the organization and its decision-making process. We arranged an away-day for the group, and I began, as I usually do, by asking people to introduce themselves and say something about the particular issue or dilemma that was bothering them about their place in the staff team. As we went around the room, it was clear that the newer members of the group neither felt they fully belonged nor understood how decisions were made, whereas the older members spoke of the importance of their history and the friendships that had built up over many years and bound people together. The newer people were saying things like: "I feel new. I don't know how the group operates as friends and colleagues" or "I don't know how to be a part of the old group." Those who had been around longer said: "I felt more connected in the past, and I'm not sure how we go forward" and "I stayed in the organization for friendships as much as anything."

I listened for the dilemmas that pointed towards an organizational discourse that would be supported by the values in the culture of the organization, and I came up with a discourse that I labelled: "Friendships are important to feel one belongs to the organization." This seemed to incorporate values that may have been important when the organization was established some thirty years earlier and, to some extent, was still an important value. But when I spelt it out as an important discourse, it then became possible to create a semantic polarity within this discourse that would be something like:

I have strong friendships in the organization	I have "not so strong" friendships in the organization

I put this on a flip chart and asked each of the group to mark in turn where they thought their position would be. This confirmed what had been presented in their introductions: long-serving members towards the left and the newer members on the right. This allowed all the member to place themselves on the polarity, and when they did this they seemed to recognize two things: (1) it was apparent that the group was spread apart, and this directed the team to think about how they worked together, and (2) it seemed to crystallize how important friendships were and that they would have to be addressed in some way to enable the team to feel more inclusive.

We continued talking about their aim of clarifying how the group could work together to plan for their future. I asked at one point whether, if the "friendship" discourse was crucial in the early days of setting up a new organization, perhaps now a new discourse, based on different values, would be more appropriate for the task of future development thirty years on. They agreed but hoped that they would never lose the value of friendship; this allowed the group to experiment with new discourses that expressed newer values. After some discussion, they came up with this: "belonging can be related to the ability to organize relevant courses". So we tried it out. I suggested a new polarity to support this discourse, and I put the two anchor points on the flip chart:

Am associated with highly relevant, successful courses	Am associated with less relevant, less successful courses

I wasn't prepared for the powerful impact that positioning themselves on this polarity had on the group. First of all, the distribution was very different from that on the "friendship" polarity. Both long-serving and newer people placed themselves at the poles. And the ensuing discussion had a more edgy and competitive feel than the one about the friendship polarity. There seemed to be more at stake regarding taking a position and being positioned by others. After all, if one delivered a course that was not successful, the "belonging" to the organization could be jeopardized. Issues of power also came to the surface, with comments like, "who has the power to say my course is less relevant than someone else's?" Who indeed. The group could only answer this by discussing the criteria for making such decisions and the organizational structure required to take these important executive decisions. After some time, they could all appreciate that this discussion was central to having a successful future.

During the afternoon, someone made the comment, "Why aren't the changes we discuss maintained after away-days?" I took this seriously (since I have asked that question myself many times) and decided to end the day with further discussion in small groups about what needed to happen in order to maintain the direction they had set during the day. They decided to organize a more clearly defined executive group and to have more frequent meetings for this group, charged with the task of addressing questions as about, for example, what will make a successful course; who is best placed to deliver it; and how they can best integrate the need for friendships with the need to develop this new discourse about the future.

Comment

In this piece of work, I am most interested in the impact that the comparison of two discourses, and their semantic polarities, had on the individuals and the focus of the team. It was dramatic; I think the simple, yet powerful, act of physically and publicly representing their positions on two contrasting polarities, one straight after the other, contributed to the group seeing things a bit differently and finding some motivation to act on the basis of the new discourse.

CASE 16
Jumping to many different positions

A social worker reflects on her feeling of being trapped in one position, and she shifts to being able to jump to several positions within the polarity. This case clearly shows how her feelings leave her positioned in one place, and through this consultation she begins to shift from tired and confused to energized and focused.

MG was asked to consult with a group of social workers working with children and young people. One of the participants said that she was confused and tired because she was going directly from the consultation to her office to meet with a 12-year-old girl who had been moved into an institution for troubled children. The girl had been subjected to ill-treatment and had been through an abortion while in the institution. The purpose of the meeting was to plan for her to be sent home to her parents.

I asked the social worker what she thought was the most important issue for her, and she said she had no problem with the meeting concerning the plans for the girl's return home, but she did not know how she was going to deal with her own feelings. She wanted to discuss what she could do to control and manage her own feelings and thoughts about being a mother and about her own little children. I said that she had given herself a polarity, and then I drew it on the flip chart and asked her to position herself on the polarity. She positioned herself on the line at A:

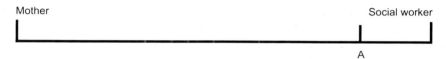

Then I asked her to put up three statements about what could be positive about having feelings that would position her closer to the "mother" end of the polarity. First, she said nothing about it was good. I insisted, and slowly she came up with three statements. She was amazed, because she had not seen anything positive in that position.

Then I asked her to make three statements about what was good in reacting in the *social worker position*. And at once she came up with four statements. I pointed out that to keep both sides balanced, she would have to come up with one more statement for the *mother position*. With a smile she said that this was not fair, and I only did this because I wanted her to like the *mother position*. I smiled back but insisted on her coming up with one more statement. She smiled again and came up with the fourth statement about what was good in reacting in the *mother position*. Then I asked her to position herself again on the line. She smiled and went up to the flip chart and started to position herself in several positions (B) on the line:

She explained that during the conversation about what was positive in both positions, she had felt that it was all right to feel both as a mother and as a social worker. She had felt free; she could see the advantages of both positions, and she intended to use it at the meeting. She seemed to be at ease in her way of positioning herself, and she, for her own part, was looking forward to ending the consultation and going back to the office to talk to the girl.

Comments

Semantic polarities enable a client to see possibilities between the poles of the polarity and not just the meanings of one or the other pole position. The relation between the positions, coupled with the possibility of having both or several positions, is important. We often see that the ease with which you may move between positions brings about energy and drive, which are both very important in carrying out any kind of tasks successfully.

And finally . . .

The telephone rang. I answered it.

"Marianne Grønbæk speaking."

"I am from *Børsen* [a financial newspaper]. Your husband has been offered a subscription, and he told me he is a manager and you are a management consultant. I mentioned some books about management that we sell, and he suggested I gave you a ring."

"Well, I'm not that interested right now. I am too busy to read for the time being."

"Why don't I send you the books now, and then you can read them later when your schedule is not so tight?"

"Well, thanks, but no thank you, I'm really not interested!"

"Well, I could give them to you on approval, and then you can decide whether to keep them or send them back."

"Well, I am not interested right now. You see, I am in the process of writing a book myself, a book for managers about positions in organizations. And right now, I don't want to be disturbed in my writing by reading other books."

"So you are writing a book on management! How interesting!"

"Yes. In fact, I am writing about exactly what we are doing in our conversation right now. I mean taking positions: you have your arguments and I have mine. We'll never get to each other in this way. You have your special offer for me that I can buy some books from you—but let me take the opposite position and make you an offer: you can buy my book when it is finished. So you see, we both want to convince each other about our exceptional offer. I might be interested in your books at a later time."

Then she replied, "And I am very interested in buying and reading your book when it is finished. So why don't I contact you in April and then we can talk further."

We both laughed and said "Until then!" and that we were looking forward to talking again.

Comment:

Being aware of the use of positions can stimulate many new conversations and new relationships. It is up to us to play with positions and with each other in the spaces created between the positions.

CHAPTER SEVEN

Exercises

People learn in many ways, and we have tried to find different approaches to conveying the central ideas behind the Semantic Polarities model. The two settings in which we are most often presenting our ideas are consultation to organizations and training other professionals, and we have, over the years, designed a number of exercises that help people understand and absorb the Semantic Polarities concepts, to get them "under your skin". Some of the exercise presented here have been used with client organizations, others come from training workshops, and they represent a different opportunity for learning than we have presented thus far in the book—a chance for readers to play with ideas and experiences and learn from participating directly in the process. We hope some of the readers will be interested to try these exercises themselves, with clients and colleagues, and we would be very keen to hear how they work for others and whether new exercises emerge from working with these ideas.

In order to make it easier to refer to an exercise, and to encourage a playful attitude towards this style of learning, we have given each exercise a name and added some comments about our experiences with them.

1. *Getting interested in difference*

An exercise to acquaint people
with the experience of positioning

This exercise is particularly good for introducing people to the idea of taking positions within a polarity. It is designed for people to make a personal statement about their position in a common, current topic and to experience someone else at another position within the same polarity. From the two positions, each is able to listen to the other and consider moving to a new position on the polarity. The exercise is about listening, not persuading.

We ask people to get into threesomes: two people to choose positions and one to act as moderator. The pair is asked to choose a topic on which they have two different points of view. A suggested list of topics has been put on the flip chart (though they may choose another if they wish), on the basis that these topics are controversial and are likely to generate different views. We have used such topics as:

- Divorce is too easy
- Euthanasia should be legalized
- Abortion should not be legal
- Vegetarianism is a good way to live
- Our country needs more immigrants.
- Marriage is essential for a stable society
- Drugs should be legal
- Businesses discriminate against women
- Our society is racist
- God does not exist

> 1. The pair is asked to polarize this topic with anchor points such as, "Yes, this is always correct" and "No, this is never correct", and then, by making a value statement about the topic, to clarify where they would position themselves on the polarity.

2. We then ask them to explain to each other why their
    position is important to them, but they are to refrain
    from trying to convince the other of the validity or mer-
    its of their position. Only explanations of the personal
    importance of the positions are encouraged. We talk
    about the "meaning behind the position". The modera-
    tor is asked to stop the pair if they start to persuade
    each other. (This lasts about 10 minutes.)

3. The moderator is then asked to help each of the pair to
    understand the validity of the other's position, given
    the information about the meaning and the importance
    of this position for the other.

4. The final instruction is for each to consider shifting
    their own position in a small way. The moderator helps
    them discuss "What aspects of the other's position are
    interesting to you and what aspects might you include
    if wanted to widen your perspective and shift your
    position, very slightly, in the direction of the other's
    position?" In other words, if they were going to extend
    their thinking and incorporate one idea or one aspect
    of the other's thinking, what might that be? (10 min-
    utes)

5. We end by asking them to metaphorically step back
    and, with the moderator's help, to discuss what they
    learned about positioning and dialogue from this ex-
    ercise. (5–10 minutes)

2. Tug of war

An exercise to create a dialogue
in a process of understanding

We have used this exercise, in different settings, to introduce
working with Semantic Polarities. It is designed for people to
experience the relation between a statement and a position.
Once the relation is visualized, it gives people a chance to relate

to their own statement and then they can feel free to take other positions within the polarity.

The exercise is divided into two parts. The first part is drawing out the polarity line on the flip chart and creating conversations around the positions on the polarity line. The second part is the conversation about the exercise.

It is a spontaneous exercise, in that any statement from a person can be used. The statement is put up at one end of a polarity line, and we make the opposite statement, placing it at the other end of the line; if an opposite statement is not obvious to us, we may ask the person what he or she thinks should be the opposite statement. We just use the spontaneous statement and put up the opposite statement.

Part one:

1. The exercise may be "triggered" by something that is said in the course of a consultation or training event. It is usually some remark or comment that stands out as being different from the general flow of conversation—something out of place, or surprising, or impolite. We catch the statement and write it on the flip chart at one end of a polarity line (Position A). At the other end we put the opposite statement (Position B).

2. We ask the person, now in Position A, to "sit back" and let the other participants work.

3. We ask the rest of the group to talk in threesomes about what is positive in both positions. We want this phase to be short, so we give 10 minutes to this conversation.

4. We ask the threesomes to tell the plenary group what they have been talking about, and we write all the statements on the flip chart. Statements about what is good about the A statement are written underneath the A position. Statements about what is good in the B statement are written underneath the B position.

5. We ask the person who made the statement to look at the polarity line and tell us where he or she now positions him/herself on the polarity and talk about the reasons for this (new) position. Then the group also take new positions and give their reasons.

Part two:

6. We invite all the participants to discuss the exercise— what it made them think about positions, about relations, and about the use of Semantic Polarities.

Our experiences

It is not necessary for A to change his or her position. The value of this exercise is to create a better dialogue in a wider context of understanding and to get to understand the concept of positions.

3. Positions please

An exercise to position oneself in one's organization

We have used this simple exercise in a training workshop consisting of a range of managers who wanted to learn about the Semantic Polarities model.

Each member of the group is asked to identify three or four important polarities within their own organization and then to position themselves on the polarity. Once the positions have been identified, we ask them to present this to a partner and work with the partner to speculate about (a) how they remain fixed where they are as a result of the different positions taken by others on the same polarity; and (b) whom would they create a dialogue with if they wanted to move to another position. (This exercise takes about 15 minutes per person. Since it is important to do it with a partner, this means about 30 minutes overall.)

4.   The apple

An exercise to clarify questions asked from the C-position

This exercise is particularly effective for helping people learn to ask good questions from the C-position. The C-position is a moderator's position and does not have a position on the polarity line that is represented by A and B. The C-position is about listening to the conversation between the two persons taking the A and B positions, and it is our experience that this can be very difficult.

We use this exercise to work with the C-position and the questions that can be asked from this position. To assist in feeling the position and focusing on good questions, we make use of an object such as an apple. It is our experience that an apple can be a visible sign of "who's in charge" of the thinking that will bring new meaning to the problem. The weight and the visibility of the apple encourage an awareness of being in the C-position and remind C to stay in that position and concentrate on asking open and process-creating questions.

We ask people to work in pairs (the A- and C-positions), facing one another. C begins by holding the apple in his or her hand. We instruct people that every time a question is asked, C must offer the apple to A, who is only to take the apple if it is a good question—that is, a question that stimulates many reflections for A. After answering a question, A gives the apple back to C.

We ask the pairs to work like this for 15 minutes. Then they must swap positions so that A takes the C-position and C takes the A-position, and they work for another 15 minutes. We emphasize that they must work for the whole period of 15 minutes because we know that often it is very hard to formulate good questions to ask from the C-position.

For second part of the exercise, we give new instructions:

1.   A must find a small problem and describe her or his position in the problem. It can be helpful to think: Why is it a problem for A?

2.   A tells the problem to C and gives the apple to him or her. C takes the apple.

3. C now tries to ask questions that stimulate reflection. Each time a question is being asked, C hands the apple to A.

4. A is to take the apple only if the question is activating A's understanding of the problem and creating new understanding. A must *not* take the apple if it is only a yes-or-no question.

5. A gives the apple back to C when answering a question.

6. C then must ask a new question.

7. After 15 minutes, A and C change positions by changing seats, and the exercise starts over again.

We end this exercise by inviting A and C to discuss which questions worked for A in the process of understanding the problem in new ways, which questions worked for C in the process of being aware of asking questions, and what sort of questions seemed to work well for C.

Our experiences

It can also be helpful for C to ask several closed and leading questions in order to feel and move forward in the process of asking good questions.

5. Gold digging

An exercise to clarify important discourses in the organization

We have designed this exercise to help people to get into conversations about important issues in the organization. In organizations, some issues are more talked about than others, and some are never talked about. There is a tendency of repeating the conversations about a few issues and of people getting stuck in the positions in these issues. The exercise puts the themes into a good dialogue, which changes the atmosphere in the organization in a positive way.

We use this exercise to extend the number of issues. When we start to talk about further issues, we are given the opportunity to choose the most important ones. By choosing a new issue, we can invite people to a new conversation, where they are freer to take new positions in the conversations.

We want people both to work with the "old" important issues and to be creative and free to find new important issues. Then we want people to create polarity lines, and finally we want them to take positions within the polarity lines. At the end we are inviting the entire group to a conversation about the possibilities of having many different issues and how to create conversations that bring the important issues into practice.

The exercise is a process. It is important that everybody is invited into and is joining the conversations. So we arrange the exercise as a process with three parts:

---

1. We ask people to form groups of four participants, sitting in a circle facing each other, without a table.

    a. We ask them to start with 5 minutes of silence. Each person thinks about and writes down the most important issue he or she can think of. We tell them it is a process and ask them to allow themselves to spend the entire 5 minutes thinking and writing and that it is OK to stay with the first issue or to change to a second or a third.

    b. Then we ask the groups to start a process in which, taking turns, each person in the group will say what she or he thinks is the most important issue in the organization, then lean back and listen to and reflect on what the other three people are talking about. Then that person tells what has been most meaningful to her or him in the conversation between the other three persons:

(i) Each round consists of one person stating her or his important issue an d then leaning back and listening. This person cannot participate in the conversation.

(ii) The other three talk about what polarity lines they can create within the issue. They will draw all the polarity lines on a piece of paper visible to everyone in the group while talking about the lines.

(iii) The person reflects on which of the polarity lines she or he thinks is interesting or important and why. The three other persons cannot interfere in the person's reflections.

(iv) Each of the four rounds takes 15 minutes. And before a new round, everybody has to change position by changing seats.

2. We ask the entire group what would be the best discourse and polarity line(s) to bring positive changes into the organization, and how this can be done in the best way.

3. Finally, we ask what the group think has been the most important thing that has happened in the exercise, and how they can use that in a constructive and positive way in the organization.

Our experiences:

To make the group stay in the creative process for a bit longer than they normally are, it is important to tell the groups that they must use all the time even if they think they could do it in less time.

6. *The devil and the angel*

An exercise to clarify the power of one's own thoughts in conflicts

It is not at all unusual to see energy channelled into a conflict. The energy often lies in a person saying what he or she does not like about another. Frequently this turns out to be because one only sees what another person has prevented one from doing, or how the other has done something that has caused problems.

We do not attempt to pursue the issue of whether this is right or wrong; rather, this exercise is done merely to create new thoughts so that the person can feel freer in the way he or she is thinking about this other person. It channels energy in a different direction to help people think in a different way.

The exercise requires a participant and an interviewer; the latter is told to stick closely to Position C and not to get into a discussion about right or wrong with the interviewee.

Because the exercise involves sharing personal issues, we ask people in the group to get together with another person they would like to share these thoughts with. When the group has formed pairs, we give the instructions for the exercise:

1. The two persons are to sit facing each other.

2. The two persons must decide which of them is taking the A-position (telling) and which is taking the C-position (interviewing).

3. A now tells about a conflict with someone and what the conflict is about.

4. C draws out a polarity line on a flip chart or a piece of paper and puts A's name at one end of the line (Position A) and the name of the other person in the conflict at the opposite end of the line—the B-position.

5. C asks A the following questions pointing at the B-position on the flip chart and writing down A's answers below Position B on the polarity line:

   a. What has this person made possible for you?

    b. What have you learned from your relationship with this person?

    c. How have the differences between the two of you been good for you in your personal life/in your work?

6. C points at the polarity line and both positions and asks A these questions:

    a. *Which new thoughts do you now have about this person?*

    b. *What changes have this exercise made in your relation with this person?*

    c. *How will this person recognize these changes?*

7. Now A and C switch positions, both mentally and physically by changing chairs.

8. The exercise is repeated (from Point 3 to Point 6)

It is important to let people take their time in this exercise. That means 30 or 45 minutes for each person. After the exercise we ask the entire group what has been good in the exercise and how they will be able to use the experience in the organization.

Our experiences:

This exercise is very important for organizations. Through these conversations, people feel freer and more energetic about acting differently.

7. Identifying discourses

An exercise to clarify the many discourses that are contained in one position

This exercise is designed as a way of exploring discourses. In some situations, people seem to get stuck because they have one way of thinking about a problem. With the help of other people's reflections, they can be enabled to see the complexity of their thoughts in a simple way. From there they can choose what discourse they want to work with first, second, and so on.

In order to set people free and strengthen the creative process, we emphasize that this exercise is only about changing one's way of thinking. It is important in the reflections not to talk about solutions and only to create as many discourses as possible.

We start the exercise by drawing an "empty" polarity line (without any statements at the ends) on the flip chart. Then we mention that at each end/position there are many discourses and show this on the flip chart:

People are then asked to work in threesomes. We suggest that they choose people they do not know too well, or those with whom they do not work too closely, or those whom they find different from themselves. We explain that sometimes it is easier to talk with or listen to people we don't know too well, that sometimes we listen more carefully to "new" people's "new" words, and that this is helpful in this exercise.

When they have moved into threesomes, we instruct them about the exercise:

1. They take it in turns for one person to be in Position A, while the other two form a reflecting team.

2. One person at time, from Position A, tells about a situation in which they identify a problem for themselves in the organization and the position they see themselves taking. For example, one situation might be: *"how we should do our work as nurses in a department of a large hospital which has had to cut back. I am the head nurse in the department."*

3. A describes the situation then "sits back" and listens to the other two people's reflections about all the differ-

ent discourses they can think of from what A just told them. These two are not to discuss the discourses but just to find as many as they can for 10 minutes. While they are talking they should write the discourses down on a flip chart or a large piece of paper.

4. After the 10 minutes of open reflection, A reads the discourses and talks for 10 minutes about her or his reflections on the discourses, inspired by these questions:

    a. Which discourses could be effective/helpful to put into dialogues in my organization?

    b. Which discourses would not be effective /unhelpful to put into dialogues in my organization?

5. After the 10 minutes, A briefly reflects on what has been good for her or him doing this exercise.

6. The next person in the group now takes Position A, and the exercise is repeated.

When the threesomes have finished their work, we ask the entire group to share thoughts about what has been interesting doing the exercise. We talk about and gather all the new learning we can think of.

Our experiences:

As the exercise goes on, people seem to find it easier to release themselves from the first thought given from the A-position, and they get more and more creative. In this process, people tell us that it gets easier with the second and third person in the threesomes. They tell us that the conversation itself about the many discourses actually "sets them free", in the sense that they feel more creative and learn to "see the matter from many angles". They say that they can also use this exercise for themselves in their personal reflections.

CHAPTER EIGHT

Being a consultant

I n a recent seminar, David was asked how he constructs a consultation. This relevant question gave us the idea for each of us to reflect on the ways we are putting the model into the practice of consultancy. This chapter offers a range of ideas, from the way requests come to us, to how we formulate problems, to how we maintain our role as consultants. Readers, however, have to remind themselves that this is an up-to-the-minute account of our respective work. We are both consultants who highly value development; in fact, the Semantic Polarities model has been elaborated through such development. It is our hope that this development will continue, and we invite readers to use these ideas in their own way to elaborate their own practice.

Organizing a consultation (from DC)

Managers are embedded in their organizations. Demands are made from managers, leaders, and directors above them in the hierarchy, from colleagues at their own level, and from staff below. These demands are presented to the manager in the form of requests to do something specific or solve a specific problem, but they are always more complicated. They are also about the people who make the requests and the particular agendas they have for making the request in the first place. So to really understand what a specific request means, in order to make the best response, the manager would do well to understand something of the unspoken, implicit agendas behind the request. This is very difficult to do in the work-a-day world where so much is happening simultaneously and in a political climate in which people may not be inclined to reveal the full meaning behind their requests.

Using the Semantic Polarities model enables managers to focus their attention on the notion that there will be myriad values underpinning the culture of the organization. Some will be about serving clients or customers, some will be about personal advancement, some will be about how office politics should be conducted. The values can be represented as discourses from which meanings are constructed. This means that a manager can step back and consider a colleague's behaviour as a position in relation to other positions within the discourse. Seeing a range of positions in the larger context of discourses and meanings is a way for an embedded manager to step back and see things in a wider perspective. Managers also tell us about the challenges of managing other people. This model is a way to help people see other options for their work and their future development because their work is placed in a continuum, and that brings other positions into view.

Requests for help come to us in all sorts of ways, and the structure of a consultation is guided by the presenting problem and the way it is presented by the client. Although we do not have routine ways of setting up a consultation, and there are probably differences between the way each author would answer this question, we have tried in this section to spell out some ideas that can be useful because they offer a framework for managing what can be a very complex process. Our systemic thinking leads us to observe feedback and modify the structure of a consultation from beginning to end. We start by meeting a client to listen to their concerns and the way the concerns are presented. We try to observe both content and process. For example, we assume that our client's presentation of the problem represents his or her position among many possible positions, which helps us think immediately about other positions and stories-not-told.

We use a metaphor of concentric circles to hold the levels of the organization in mind as we talk to the client, such as this:

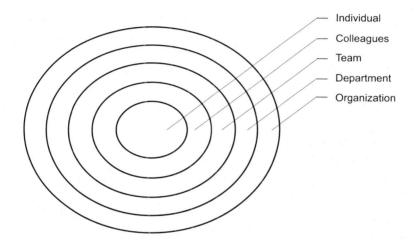

— Individual
— Colleagues
— Team
— Department
— Organization

The client will present an issue, and we can initially locate this in one of the concentric circles. For example, "I have a staff member who is seen as overly critical when she communicates with others", would be located near the centre of the circle, as opposed to a problem such as, "our organization is struggling between the forces of centralization and localization", which locates the presenting problem in the outer circles. But, of course, systemic consultants will want to move back and forth among the levels to see the problem "systemically". However, the presentation helps us know where to start. We might negotiate the work with one person, two colleagues, a team, or parts of the whole organization.

Our model is well suited to consulting to individuals and can be usefully applied in coaching, mentoring, and role consultation. Many of our consultations begin by asking an individual to place her/himself and colleagues on relevant polarities.

The model is also well suited to smaller-sized groups (i.e. 5–20), which allow us to engage everyone in using Semantic Polarities and starting new conversations. If the scope of our assignment is large, it can be difficult to locate everyone within the same polarities or focus their attention on the positions that are important to colleagues. In a larger organization we might do some do some work with smaller groupings and then link the experiences of diverse groups to the polarities that are important for the whole organization.

We often find ourselves working with smaller organizations, teams, or departments (5–20 people) and with individuals or pairs who are locked in conflict. We use different types of discussions of polarities and positions to move towards greater dialogic communication. The reader will gather from the case studies that dialogic communication can be used with one person or several people or can be established as a value and activity for an entire organization.

Organizing a consultation (from MG)

The most important thing about the Semantic Polarities model is the dialogue that this tool enables you to generate. I use Semantic Polarities to create an open space for conversations about issues that feel most important to members of staff and managers in an organization.

The dialogues are the heart and the spark of life not only in the consultation, but also in the organization. The dialogues form the relations that will support and develop the whole organization. The relations reflect and are reflected by the dialogues that are going on and may be created in an organization.

The dialogues are essential to me and help in defining me as a consultant. I measure myself by the importance of the dialogues I can help to create in the organizations where I work.

When I am contacted by an organization, I have a conversation with the manager about the issues he or she wants to have discussed. We lay down the overall framework, the overall discourse for the agreement. The time and place for the arrangement is laid down as well.

At the consultation, the manager and I start by outlining the framework, and then I invite those present to talk in groups about which issue they think is the most important one to discuss within the discourse that has been outlined. I write down all their suggestions on a flip chart. At this point I use the discourse we have agreed upon to stick to the context of the conversation. If some of the participants wish to take up issues outside the discourse, I may "reject" them from referring to the agreed discourse, but I may also try to involve the manager in an open dialogue about the possibility of expanding or, in some cases, opening the overall discourse. I do this by asking the manager and the staff members if it is possible to arrange a conversation about some of the issues inside the overall discourse.

All participants are involved in choosing the issues they think of as most important. I write the particular discourses in question on a flip chart and draw the semantic polarity lines connected with each of them. I invite the participants to join me in outlining the polarities. I ask them to talk about which statements they suggest should be put at the ends of the polarity. I do this by arranging the conversations in groups or by having a conversation in the open with the person or persons who seem to have the problem, the challenge, or the wish for change. It often happens that the participants only think about the statement at one end of the polarity. So I invite them to talk together or with me about what to put at the other end.

It is my experience that drawing out semantic polarities is a very effective way of creating good conversations among the participants, which, as mentioned above, is a very important object.

A little story:

> In a staff development consultation with the members of a department consisting of several groups, I was working with one group at a time, while the other groups were in a circle outside, reflecting on the process going on in the group that was inside talking with me. This group was said to have so many and such

large differences that they were unable to agree on very much. I started the conversation with the group by showing them four flip-chart pens in different colours and asking them which colour they wanted me to use. They took turns to pick a pen, and each time I took the pen that each of them chose. It did not take long before I was holding all four pens in my hand. I asked the question again, and the same thing happened, only this time they put more energy into their arguments. I asked again, and this time they were all very active, arguing for their colours. Then I showed them one of the pens and asked all of those who had not wanted that particular colour what they thought was good about the arguments put forward by those who wanted this colour. They said what they had heard the "fans" of this colour say. I repeated the procedure with the other three colours, and then I asked again which colour they wanted me to use. Now the arguments were fewer and less persistent, and the participants were listening more and more to each other. And now they were able to pick a colour because they had heard each other. Some of the people in the outside circle commented that this was a lot of time spent on coloured pens. I said that we could state that at one end of a polarity. At the other end we could write what I had noticed: the group is working with and listening to each other. We laughed and played on a little with the process they had been through, and then we started talking about the issue the group had chosen. They carried on being attentive about listening to each other, and they experienced a new and pleasanter way for them to have conversations.

I want to underline here that I do think that what we talk about is important. The discourses and polarities we choose *are* very important to the dialogues. The dialogues are essential both to and during the processes of change. The story merely makes us aware of the fact that change can be brought about in many ways and through many different kinds of talks and issues. Therefore, I find it useful to involve the participants in lining out polarities as well as discourses. The dialogue itself helps to create a secure and confident base for the discussions, for the consciousness of one's own and the others' positions, and for the processes of change.

The consultation passes off in several loops—repetitions. When one process is finished, new processes start with new discourses and polarities. Continuously, together with the participants, I identify which new thoughts, solutions, and possibilities of development can be put to work. As a consultant I often choose to express my observations and reflections. Sometimes it is of value that I contribute to the conversations with general information out of my experience or knowledge. If I do so, in the same breath I ask the participants to talk about the relevance of my ideas and to reject them if they are not relevant.

All thoughts are taken into consideration about new issues or in which way these thoughts are giving new meaning to the overall discourse and framework of that particular consultation.

Often I hang up a "learning board" on which we collect all these valuable thoughts. The "learning board" is an extra sheet from the flip chart. It offers all the participants the opportunity to join in making conclusions and agreements.

If there is a conflict, I work from the starting point that, as a consultant, I am not supposed to solve the conflict, but to bring about the open space for a dialogue in which disagreement is possible and differences are appreciated. The first thing I do is to draw out a polarity and invite both parties involved to talk about their thoughts about the conflict. Then I follow the phases from the model of conflict solving. During all the phases, I keep track of the time. There are now rules for "the right time", but I constantly assess the time and its influence on what happens in the dialogue between the two parties. In consultations of conflict solving, I underline the importance of allowing disagreements and I stress the importance of having differences in an organization. At the end of the conversation, I ask the parties to talk about how this consultation will influence their future cooperation.

Sometimes I do something quite different and unsystematized. It happens when I realize that something else can be done or needs to be done. Then it is up to my creativity to bring about what is necessary at the moment.

Towards the end of the consultation, I let the participants talk about what has been most important to them personally and to their organization. We write that down on the flip chart in the plenary session.

At the very end, I ask them what has been the best or pleasantest experience for each of them today. This is done in a final round during which the individual statements cannot be commented on. The basis for this last round is to appreciate the time we have spent together. It gives each participant the opportunity to express his or her appreciation of having received something from or having contributed to the day's work and the other participants. This round is not an evaluation of the consultant, but a way of saying thanks for the good company and for the common achievements.

I am working long-term consulting in a number of organizations. In these organizations, I use "rituals" or routines so that the participants are helping to create the session themselves. In my mind, there is a connection between this and the way I involve the participants and make them responsible when we draw out the semantic polarities. The advantage of routines lies in the fact that the participants feel familiar with the procedure and feel that they have an influence on and a responsibility for the success of the consultation. The disadvantage is that the participants may place more attention on form than on content. I am always very aware of that, and if it happens, I may choose to involve them in my thoughts and change the routines.

Routines develop through repetitions. Repetitions create recognition. I experience how the organizations, through the repetitions, elaborate the ability to use the methods on an everyday basis, which has a positive and constructive effect on their conversations and their cooperation. One of my clients said in an interview:

> "I think 'Semantic Polarities', and I automatically know that there are always at least two positions, two viewpoints, two opinions. The Semantic Polarities model is a tool that makes management easier."

Using the model for strategic and relational issues

In our view, the Semantic Polarities model stimulates organizational development at the level of ideas and the level of personal commitment to the organization. It enables an organization to generate ideas that are informed by many perspectives or positions. This means that the final decision is more robust and more able to respond to a diverse environment because the process of arriving at the decision was one of addressing diversity and including it within the final decision.

The model also enables the individuals in the organization to feel connected to the process of change. We find that the more they are connected and the more they feel their own ideas are being heard and considered within the final decision, the more employees will take a personal interest in the development of the organization. Ultimately organizational efficiency improves when the employees want to modify their own behaviour or the breadth of their own vision for the good of the organization as a whole.

When used as a method for addressing communication between individuals and/or members of a team, it is clear to us that the model contributes to the creation of a safe environment by depersonalizing misunderstandings and conflicts and setting down clear, neutral, respectful ground rules for ways people can develop new ways of seeing each other and connecting to each other. The model is relational, and thereby anyone who has felt marginalized and undervalued finds that his or her behaviour is described in a relation to other people's behaviour in the organization. Feeling connected in this way makes it easier for people to venture into a new conversation.

CHAPTER NINE

The client's voice

Justine Grønbæk Pors

Justine Grønbæk Pors is a student of organizations at the Department of Business Studies at Roskilde Universitycenter, Denmark. She is also Marianne's daughter and, through her, has attended several seminars and consultation work based on Appreciative Inquiry and Semantic Polarities.

I have always played with the metaphor that relationships are like people connected with string. These strings have different lengths, thicknesses, and forms as they hold people together. Since I study organizational culture and I work as a supervisor for teachers of physical education, there are strings that connect me to many different professional conversations. I have also observed in my mother's work how she untangles organizational knots, and I have watched the way the strings between these people grew stronger and stronger while the knots were untied.

As part of the research for this book, I had the privilege of visiting different organizations who have been working with Semantic Polarities. I interviewed managers first of all to throw light on their experiences, to bring the reader closer to the organizations and the people who are using this model and experiencing successes and challenges in relation to their work.

I have given considerable thought to way the interviews may be affected by my interviewing clients about work done by my own mother! On the one hand, as I look back over the interviews, I believe that some of the honesty and trust the persons interviewed showed me might be generated by the fact that I reminded them of my mother, with whom they have shared the whole working process. It felt as though I was able to step right into the context, and I found it very easy to get the people I interviewed to remember good and bad situations regarding their work. I think I profited by the combination of knowing about Semantic Polarities and also being able to ask curious and open questions since I had not been involved in the consultation process that took place in each organization.

On the other hand, it may be more difficult for me to be "objective" in the way this concept is used in traditional scientific research. Also, my position could have prevented the persons interviewed from sharing with me their frustrations and problems with the model and their ways of working, because they felt unable to say something bad about the process that my mother had been involved in. Clearly these factors have some impact on the validity of the findings, but my overriding impression is that these experienced managers were very well able to recall their problems as well as their successes.

How can one evaluate the organizational work done with Semantic Polarities? We were not interested in testing with yes/no answers whether the model of Semantic Polarities is a good tool for organizational development. We wanted to get a better understanding of how the people from the different organizations had experienced the working process. And we wished to make use of all the valuable experiences of the people who have worked with this tool.

We believed that the data that would be useful in developing the understanding of organizational work were to be found not in numbers but in the specific experiences and in the many ways that the organizations have adjusted the methods of Semantic Polarities to each of their special situations.

In creating the interview guide as well as in the situation of the interviews, I found Kvale (1996) and his thoughts on the qualitative research interview very helpful. With Kvale in mind, and with help from David, I made the interview guide semi-structured and full of open-ended questions, so that I could be assured of rich, specific, spontaneous answers from the person being interviewed (Kvale, 1996).

As the intention with the conversations was to clarify the specific practice in a particular organization as experienced by the people involved, I tried to adapt the questions to the particular context of the location, the type of organization, and the person being interviewed. And I sought to pursue and clarify the meaning of the subjects that I sensed were important to that person.

I carried out six interviews in all, three of which are presented in this chapter. The other three are my safety-belt to ensure that the three presented ones are not exceptional. The persons interviewed are all former clients of Marianne's.

The persons interviewed differ in terms of age, gender, and personality, but they are all managers or deputies in their respective organizations. We selected these particular persons because of their long-term experience with organizational development in general and, more specifically, with Semantic Polarities. We decided to talk to these managers because they have been involved in the whole process, including choosing to work with this model rather than other approaches in the market.

So we wanted to ask the experts—the people who are seeking to implement the theory in their working practices, their relationships, and their dialogues—to step back and reflect on the work they had done with Semantic Polarities over a longer period of time.

It is my hope that readers will enjoy the stories and valuable experiences as much as I did and perhaps will even recognize some issues and situations from their own organizational work.

Interview 1

I am sitting with Lisa, the female deputy of an institution for nine physically and mentally disabled adults, located on an island in the south of Denmark. I arrived one morning after breakfast and met the residents getting ready to do their everyday business. A few of the thirty staff members assist the residents where it is needed. They are all trained teachers or health care assistants.

I am there to talk to Lisa about her work with Semantic Polarities. I ask her to remember when she was first taught about the Semantic Polarities model and when she first tried to use it in her organization.

"In the beginning it was hard. You had to understand it yourself. But the more you do it, the easier it gets. When I spoke about it theoretically, it met with opposition. They [i.e. the staff members] had to see it in action and see it work before it became something they wanted to work with."

"What was the opposition about?"

"It was the exercise where you discover the good things about the position of the other. That was hard. 'Why do we have to do that?' they said. Here it was not about your own opinions; it was about the other's. And saying something good about the other's opinion—how was that going to help?"

"So when did you and your employees realize that this is not just theory?"

"I remember a situation when I thought, okay, now we have to make a choice: we are going to try using Semantic Polarities. It was an incident in the staff group about whether you could bring your dog to work or not. It was a conflict between two persons, and the issue was separating the staff into groups for and against. I consciously decided that now was the time to use Semantic Polarities! I put the line with the theme of the conflict up on the whiteboard, and we did the exercise of asking each staff member to indicate their position and then discuss the process together.

You can bring your dog to work

You cannot bring your dog to work

"It was tough! But afterwards I asked around among the staff how it had been, and they said that it worked really well. Among other things, they said that the discussions became much more varied and balanced for the persons listening. Now you were not just for or against each other. Previously we had a tendency not to look so much at the issue, but to choose which person to agree with. Now they—we all—began to see something good in what both the persons involved in the conflict were saying, and then we were able to take a stand. Before we started the exercise, we had reached a point where the members of staff were really stuck. Now we could talk about it again.

"Later we brought it up again, and people were able to be honest. Now it was about the issue itself. You had the courage to be honest, because it was no longer a personal matter. All the way around the table, people dared to speak out about their opinion. In a group you may easily find that you have the same opinions as the people you like, but all of a sudden everybody had the courage to say and mean something about both positions.

"That is my most clear memory. The first time we really used Semantic Polarities."

"Tell me about other areas where you find this working tool useful!"

"It is really useful for illustrating where you position yourself as a group of staff in relation to practically anything.

"We have had a lot of criticism from the residents' parents about practical aspects of their care. In the beginning we had some parents who were very quick to shake their fingers at us—not over the educational process, but over the more practical things. Every time they found a bit of dust or a spot on their son's shirt, they mentioned it to us.

"So I found myself thinking that the residents had to have clean fingernails, and completely clean clothes, and the rooms had to be really shiny, even though my common sense didn't think that all these things were that important compared to so many other things. So the staff was running around like mad, cutting fingernails and making sure that all those practical things were done perfectly. And as a result, some of the more educational things failed, because we did not pay attention to them, and that was really unsatisfying.

"Then we drew a continuum on the whiteboard, with the two polarities called something like "Important to be in the house" and "Important to leave the house".

"And then we saw that many of us were positioned around the practical things in the house. I think as a manager I had driven many of the staff members with me towards that end of the line. Actually no one thought it important to have excursions and activities—all the things we now consider really important. And when we saw that, we understood what we were doing and why."

She laughs.

"But then we were able to talk about it. 'Does anybody want to move positions?' And many of us did, actually, because it is not all that satisfying cutting fingernails all the time. And then it became a conscious change, and at the same time we were able to make sure that someone stayed in the position of the 'in-house' carer.

"I have been noticing how I positioned myself and how that dragged my staff members in the same direction. So I think Semantic Polarities have made me more conscious about my leadership and about where we are going ... a more steady course and a more deliberate course."

"Is there any way in which you have modified the model or adapted it to yourself? I mean, a particular way in which it works for you?"

"Now that we have all learned this and know how to use it, it may have the effect of a red rag to a bull when in a conflict you are asked 'What is good about . . .? There is nothing good about it, damn it!'

"So in these situations I have to find some other ways of putting it. I don't ask the direct question: What is good in what he says and what he does? I try to ask in another way. We change the questions."

"So that the questions don't become predictable and disrespectful of what people are experiencing."

"Yes, because I sometimes feel that people, as I said, react to it as a red rag when they feel that now I am just doing an exercise with them. 'Now she's just doing one of her silly exercises. What good will it do now that I am so angry?'

"Then I do not refrain from using it, but I try to ask questions in a way that makes it less obvious that I'm doing it."

"To be quite specific, how do you ask, then?"

"Well, that's just what I'm thinking . . . I think what I do is, I keep asking questions. Actually, I think I just keep asking infuriatingly many questions, until they start to figure out for themselves that there might be something good about the other's position. I think that's what I do."

"But does that mean that you do not ask in a deliberately positive way? You ask neutral questions?"

"Yes, that's what I do. Because positive questions may feel provocative in a conflict. So I ask in a more neutral way—that's true, that's what I do. But I do try to stick to my focus in some way or another. I do not permit negativity to drive us around in a circle. I have to do something to break it. At some point, in the end it will untie itself. So even though I am neutral, I stick to my positive focus."

"It sounds as if you have the patience to wait until the positive thinking comes up in an honest way."

"Yes, that's what I do. I can hear that they are using it. They say, 'I know that when I act in such a way . . ., I force you to . . .' It is when it becomes a natural part of our relations that we really move."

"Do you think you will carry on using the Semantic Polarities model in future?"

"Yes, definitely. We can feel that it works. Our residents have also begun to adapt it. During the last year it has really evolved—a lot of things have happened. You can walk around in our organization and hear people saying. 'Yes, that is one position: what are the good things about that?' It has become natural for us. You don't have to think as much about it any more; it is lying around in every corner of our organization, that this is the way we do it."

Interview 2

For this interview I am visiting an organization lying in lovely surroundings in the countryside of Denmark. The institution is a home and a place of treatment for homeless people, who often have a long history of drug or alcohol abuse. The institution has capacity for thirty clients; it has a group of twelve superintendent/managers, and there are fifty members of staff in all.

The institution is especially known for a project called "It Is Possible", which has succeed in getting young boys, who had no home and were serious drug abusers, back on track. Before the boys were introduced to this institution, they had no hopes for the future; today there are stories of how they now have homes and jobs and are struggling to reach their dreams of a normal life.

So I am very keen to meet the manager, Jonas, to hear his thoughts and strategies concerning organizational development with the Semantic Polarities.

He describes the change he has experienced in his organization over the last year in particular. He tells me that they have worked with Semantic Polarities in two different forms: in individual staff-development conversations (similar to appraisal interviews) and in group development for the managers in the organization. I am keen to learn more about these specific applications of Semantic Polarities.

"Tell me how you and your staff have used Semantic Polarities."

"When we talked with the group about working using Semantic Polarities, there were two interesting dimensions: how the managers positioned themselves, and how I positioned myself in relation to them. There was a tendency that in a fair number of the discourses we were positioned in a lump in the middle.

But it was interesting to see that I had adjusted myself, so that in the cases where my managers huddled together, I was out on the side, pulling. And in the cases where we were spread out nicely, there was a tendency for me to be in the middle. So Semantic Polarities is something that makes me conscious about a picture of where I want to be as the manager in relation to my employees. And it was fascinating that we were able to talk about it and why we positioned ourselves as we did.

"We are positioned so much better this year. We are not as much in a body—I mean, we are positioned very evenly scattered, and I am positioned in the middle. In general there was a better dispersal among the employees. They covered more of the continuum and had the courage to position themselves in more outer positions. I still have to pull when I feel that we have not moved in the right direction but need to get moving, and then I am all the way out there pulling the harness. But I do not need to do that as much anymore."

"I am curious, of course: in concrete, everyday practice, what do you do to encourage the culture of differences?"

"We have some inherent differences, so what I have had to do is to work with how we exploit that we are so obviously different. The differences originate from our professional qualifications. Once these differences are settled we can play, and then Semantic Polarities enter the stage. Our common base is that each employee, and preferably residents, too, are holders of qualifications. For example, we have Michael, who is the manager of the workshop. When he positions himself between "to control" and "to set free", then he is alone in "to control". He is also the one who remembers what we usually do, and it is he who remembers what agreements we made a year and a half ago. He is our guarantee for that. In an organization or in an institution that wants to move, one could be tempted to say that he is hampering us, he holds us back. But no! Here, it is a privilege. He secures our base, so that we others can play. And here we can use Semantic Polarities: to legalize. Michael is appreciated because of his position—for, as long as he is there, we can go a bit further in the opposite direction. And we like to do that."

"I have to understand this. In which way do you work with the rela-
tions? Can you remember a situation where a light dawned on some-
one: "Oh, I can position my self here, BECAUSE you are there." Or
was it obvious to everybody from the beginning?"

"I think it became very distinct when we brought in the new
staff members this year. For example, it was the deputy who
saw the light when she positioned herself in relation to me. She
saw how we can use it in our co-work and how wonderful that
really is.

"It is a method of development. It is not a grade marking. The
individual decides the agenda for the development. It is not to
shake the foundations. The purpose is not to move Michael in
the opposite direction. But Michael may have to commit to a dialogue of how the group is represented in the positions opposite
to his. I think that is important—the understanding that it is a
development-orientated evaluation, not a threat. The heaviest
defences evolve if you are uncertain about your own base. That
is the most restrictive factor for growth and change. And here
Semantic Polarities work! I have not seen it deterring anybody.
It is what my employees find easiest to work with."

It has been clear to me from the start that I am talking to a
man of many thoughts. I am quite sure that no tool is introduced
in his organization without a lot of consideration beforehand
and evaluation afterwards. Unmistakably he has given the usefulness of Semantic Polarities a lot of thought.

"I would like some research to be done," he says. "Something
that might verify the value of Semantic Polarities. When you
position yourself, how much is coincidence and what is the
value of truth?"

At the end of our talk I ask Jonas to sum up the use of
Semantic Polarities in relation to his vision and strategy for the
organization:

"There is still a way to go from having visualized it as Semantic Polarities to making use of it in everyday strategy, because it
is not necessarily a constructive way of acting together. There is
no guarantee. It is what you make of it. You have a platform for
a constructive dialogue—how do we use this? It is not enough
to position ourselves on a continuum if the position is only to

be used for our own good. Then it is only an image of where we are. Afterwards we need to talk—how do we use this in the best possible way?

"I use Semantic Polarities to make us realize where we are in relation to where we are going. It is a kind of chart we make. The more open and accessible you can make it, the more democratic we can find and set the course."

"And the more effective, I imagine?"

"Yes, definitely. I am not especially gifted or especially educated. So if we want to do something really amazing, we need more ideas than mine alone. The more open we are, the greater the variety of ideas we get."

Interview 3

My final interview is with Laura, a manager of an institution for mentally disabled people. The organization consists of four community houses and a day-care centre. It employs some sixteen staff members, and is located in a medium-sized town in Denmark.

It is a very busy day for the manager and her staff. But we find a quiet place in her office, and she takes the time to sit down with me and talk about her special experiences with Semantic Polarities.

Laura starts by telling me that they use Semantic Polarities in staff-development conversations and in supervision. "And sometimes," she adds, "my staff use it in relation to their residents. I know that in one of my community-based residential homes, my staff use it at house meetings for the residents. If a matter is up for discussion, they try to look at what is good in one position and what is good about the other."

"To be very specific, how do you use it?"

"I use it for supervising a staff member's work with a resident or when staff members have opinions that conflict in some way. I always use the whiteboard, so I just draw . . . some of my staff members simply call it "the line". It is easier to remember than Semantic Polarities.

"It often occurs that someone says, 'Can I please get this issue up on the line.' One woman in particular on my staff is very fascinated by the line. It does something special for her. But I put on the line the important statements of the individual staff members, at one end or the other. As a starting point, we talk about where they are positioned. If it concerns two persons who do not agree or need to reach some point of understanding of each other—well, that is what it is all about: reaching some understanding of each other so that you can move. Semantic Polarities are about seeing something useful in each other's ways of thinking."

"So how do you negotiate that last part, so that the persons positioned at one end of the line can understand and see the usefulness of the position at the opposite end?"

"We talk about it and do the exercises that Marianne has taught us. We define what is good about the position at one end and what is good about the position at the other end. So we talk about all the plusses about a position.

"It is a tool for clarification. We have these advantages if we go this way, and those advantages if we go that way, and where would I position myself after we have talked about it? What becomes important? Usually you can tell from the conversation that there may be a difference between the emotional involvements at either end of the line. And we try to help the staff member to decide, 'In which direction I really want to move?'"

"Can you explain that bit about emotional involvements to me?"

"For instance, the other day all my staff and I were gathered at our weekly meeting. We were discussing a future project and how we should coordinate it; some of my staff members had a wish for all of us to spend more time meeting, but some thought that they already spent too much time in meetings. So I put up this line." She draws the line for me on a sheet of paper lying in front of her:

We should have many meetings	We should be flexible about coordinating in other ways

"Each statement and each position on the line contains some feelings," she continues. The feeling, or emotions, *behind* "we should have many meetings" could be that those staff members want us to be more together. And the feeling attached to the opposite polarity might be that the others already feel stressed enough about meetings with the ones we already have.

"When we put it up on the line like this, we can let both these emotions be heard. We discover what each position contains, and it gives the person holding the position the possibility to allow the expression of the emotions he or she has in connection to the position. Often a lot is changed when the other persons in the room get a chance to hear the emotional engagement others can have with a position."

"And then what happens? Do you stop there?"

"No. After we have talked about the different positions, we ask if anyone feels ready to move. We simply ask if anyone now feels differently. And often we all do."

"Why are you then ready to move, do you think?"

"I think once your position has been heard and acknowledged, you don't feel the importance of sticking to it any more. In our example, for instance, one member of my staff felt very keenly that we should be more flexible in our coordination. But after we had given that position time and space, she wished to move herself—because after she had felt herself heard and accommodated in her position and her feelings attached to it, she felt free to take another position."

"Now I think I understand what you mean. But then I would like to ask, how do you communicate about Semantic Polarities to your staff?"

"I always use the whiteboard, because I can see that that is effective. It is both the process of getting it up on the whiteboard, and when it is there you can relate to it in a more committed way than had it only been said out loud. It becomes visual; you can understand it and reflect on it.

"What happens? Does it create a common understanding or . . .?"

"It is important that the exact words of the person who said them are written down, because it is those words that matter:

the words that have evolved from the process of discussion. And the more that people are involved, the richer the process is. You learn what the meaning is. But you could not enter the room afterwards, look at the line, see what plusses are made, and understand it. The important thing is the process."

"How did your staff feel about it when you first introduced them to Semantic Polarities?"

"At first they didn't think too much about it, but I think the light dawned when Marianne taught it to them." Laura thinks for a while, before she continues: "One of the things that my staff noticed when we started working with Semantic Polarities was that it is not plus on the one side and minus on the other, but that it is plus on both sides. Even though they sometimes find it laborious to find the plusses, they are surprised about how many there are, when you insist that there have got to be some." She pauses again, still very thoughtful, and says, "When you put plusses here as well as in other positions, you automatically create the consciousness of nuances."

"Yes, that is very true. How do you think your staff have experienced the fact that one is allowed to change one's mind and move on the line?

"Especially in the staff development conversations, I think they have really appreciated it. 'Where am I now? And where do you I want to go?' There was not only one position, but several, so that more opportunities were created. The line illustrates it so well, because the line visualizes the possibilities. Other colleagues can see ways to develop. I think, once again, that it is partly the process and partly the visualization: to be involved in the process and to see how people develop. It creates respect. Those things are made very visible on the line."

"What do you look for? I mean, in what situations do you find Semantic Polarities usable?"

"I don't even think much about it; I just have a sense when something is suitable for putting it up on the line. I look for a continuum of some tension. When arguments are stuck, then it is usable, such as situations where a change of perspective is needed."

"What else do you find important for the process in the moment as well as implementing it in everyday practice? What culture do you wish to create? Qualities in differences, for instance?"

She smiles: "Oh yes, I am very glad you asked me that. I have worked with that exact thing ever since I started. In the beginning we were an interdisciplinary group that should do the same job. At that time that was very uncommon. With your specific education and work practice, you get a set of norms and ways of doing things that might be different from the norms and ways in other trades. We have worked a lot to create space for being different—that we have different ways of doing things. We also work a lot with accepting that we are different persons. The same words may not have the same meanings when different people use them."

"It sounds like you have tried to develop an organizational culture that supports the appreciation of differences."

"We do have a culture, yes. But, of course, sometimes you consider your own position more interesting than the positions of the others. When you have reached some kind of disagreement or conflict . . . until you get to think about it, you believe your point of view is right. You see it from your own point of view. In these situations, you do not look at it from the other's position. That is what is so splendid about Semantic Polarities—that you get the perspective of the other. Or another perspective. Yes, Semantic Polarities opens up perspectives."

"Which of your personal attitudes as a manager contributes to the process?"

"I think that it is a good tool, and that it is really helpful. So, the fact that I myself consider it worth spending time on . . . yes, the fact that I can commit to it . . . that I can stand by that there has to be something good. There has got to be something, so let us try to find it. It is something about being able to bear the wait for something more to happen."

"That is interesting. Can you go into details about that?"

"It could be that one employee sees all the plusses in one position but has trouble seeing any in another position. Then you keep inviting something more. You keep the expectation that something will come out. That spirit of expectation is in the air. What is important for us is that we keep faith that it is possible to solve the conflict, change positions, and so forth. If I am not sure that it is possible, I position myself in the doubt, and then we are far away from success."

Final comments

Following the presentation of three interviews, I am still pondering some general comments made by my interviewees that will, I hope, add emphasis to what has been already said in the book or will give the reader further perspectives on the meanings that Semantic Polarities hold for organizational work.

1. All the managers described to me how working with the model has also heightened their sense of, and ability to understand, the social processes in their organization and among their staff—not to mention the relation between manager and staff. As one put it:

   "It was of great importance to me to discover that my staff members could not step into a certain position because I was taking that position. A world of opportunities opened up when I realized this. If you are alone and stubbornly stay in your position, you make it impossible for others to be there. If I believe that I'm the only one taking responsibility for a cause, then maybe I should try to leave it for a while and see who steps into this position."

2. Several of the managers discovered how the work with Semantic Polarities is closely linked to the concept of responsibility. They noticed how their staff took more

responsibility for the organization, the group, and the work process in a whole new way. The managers also described to me how the work with Semantic Polarities made them aware of in which areas their staff were taking responsibility or in which areas they wanted to.

One of them told me:

"When you see that other persons are also taking responsibility for the organization—even though it might be in ways other than you yourself would do—a lot of energy is set free. Now I have less stress from all the things I am not."

3. When I ask them why Semantic Polarities inspire people to take responsibility, they said that it is due to the new awareness of how positions affect each other. As one described:

"When we began to realize the relations between our positions, it became more meaningful to say something. You could no longer speak without saying anything, because every statement became concrete and linked to the issue somewhere on the polarity. It became clear that something you say influences the work and well-being of others."

4. One interviewee spoke about opening up a greater awareness of nuances in and between positions. She said to me: "Working with Semantic Polarities has helped our children to get a better understanding of other people. They have begun to see that things are not just black or white, but contain different facets. Before the consultations, they saw the conflicts in which they constantly find themselves as all black or all white. You are either on my side or you are against me. But when we start to ask for the good things about arguments that they had only thought of as being against them, then they begin to see the nuances and actually position themselves above the conflict. Semantic Polarities help them and help us a lot in this process."

5. And, finally, one manager spoke about the challenge of finding the "best" discourse and polarities that really help people to shift their positions. He said, "In my experience, the hardest cases are when an old conflict is lying underneath the present disagreement, an old conflict that has been buried under more and more layers over time. Then you have to search for a while to find out where the passion is coming from. In searching for the issue that would be most helpful to put on the line, I sometimes ask, 'Are your feelings with you?' And it is about listening, I mean really listening, behind the words they are saying. I suppose it is the same in all work with human beings: listening behind the words. It's not always really about the words that are spoken."

A final thank you goes to the organizations who contributed to these interviews and to a richer understanding of Semantic Polarities.

GLOSSARY OF TERMS

Anchoring: the process of articulating two statements (or more) that represent the extreme ends of a semantic polarity and enable all other meaning statements to be placed between them on the basis of their distance from the extreme.

Being positioned: refers to being aligned to a position within a discourse by another person (also referred to as *interactive positioning*).

Dialogic communication: a particular form of verbal communication that emphasizes the ability to listen carefully to the experience of "the other", the ability to be reflexive about one's participation in the conversation, and the capacity to change one's ideas through conversation (also referred to in this book as *dialogue*).

Dilemma: a perception that one is confronted with two possible courses of action, each of which leads to an unsatisfactory outcome and results in difficulty choosing either action.

Discourse: an institutionalized process (such as media, government, education) for conveying the range of points of view or positions that cluster around a theme or topic and provide, by way of Semantic Polarities, sources of meaning for a social group. Another useful definition is provided by Burr (1995), "Discourse is used primarily in two senses: (i) to refer to a systematic, coherent set of images, metaphors and so on that construct an object in a particular way, and (ii) to refer to the actual spoken interchanges between people" (p. 184).

Positioning: through verbal or nonverbal behaviour, one aligns oneself to a particular position among many positions that are made available with the prevailing discourse about a theme, topic, or value in a social environment.

Semantic Polarities: meaning is generated by the interactive process, in language, of different points of view. This is the name given to the full range of positions available on a continuum that provides the source for different points of view.

Taking a position: refers to taking the initiative to behave in a way that aligns one with a position within a discourse (also referred to as *reflexive positioning*).

REFERENCES

Anderson, H., Goolishian, H., & Winderman, L. (1986). Problem-determined systems: Towards transformation in family therapy. *Journal of Strategic and Systemic Therapies*, 5: 1–13.

Bakhtin, M. M. (1981). *The Dialogic Imagination: Four Essays by M. M. Bakhtin*, ed. M. Holquist. Austin, TX: University of Texas Press.

Bannister, D. (Ed.) (1970). *Perspectives in Personal Construct Theory*. London: Academic Press.

Bateson, G. (1936). *Naven*. Cambridge: Cambridge University Press.

Becker, C., Chasin, L., Chasin, R., Herig, M., & Routh, S. (1995). From stuck debate to new conversation on controversial issues: A report from the Public Conversations Project. *Journal of Feminist Family Therapy*, 71 (1/2): 143–163.

Buber, M. (1970). *I and Thou*. New York: Scribner.

Burr, V. (1995). *An Introduction to Social Constructionism*. London: Routledge.

Campbell, D. (2000). *The Socially Constructed Organization*. London: Karnac.

Campbell, D., Coldicott, T., & Kinsella, K. (1994). *Systemic Work with Organizations: A New Model for Managers and Change Agents*. London: Karnac.

Campbell, D., Draper, R., & Huffington, C. (1991). *A Systemic Approach to Consultation*. London: Karnac.

Cooperrider, D. (1990). Positive imagery, positive action: The affirmative basis of organising. In S. Srivastra & D. Cooperrider (Eds.), *Appreciative Management and Leadership*. San Francisco, CA: Jossey-Bass.

Cooperrider, D., & Srivastra, S. (1987). Appreciative inquiry in organisational life. *Research in Organisational Change and Development, 1*: 129–169.

Davies, B., & Harré, R. (1990). Positioning and personhood. In: R. Harré & L. V. Langenhove (Eds.), *Positioning Theory* (chap. 3). Oxford: Blackwell, 1999.

Deetz, S. (1995). Character, corporate responsibility and the dialogue in the post-modern context. *Organization, 2* (2): 217–225.

Deetz, S. (2003). Authoring as a collaborative process through communication. In: D. Holman & R. Thorpe (Eds.), *Management and Language* (chap. 7). London: Sage.

Derrida, J. (1978). *Writing and Difference*. Chicago, IL: University of Chicago Press.

de Shazer, S. (1985). *Keys to Solution in Brief Therapy*. New York: W. W. Norton

Festinger, L. (1957). *A Theory of Cognitive Dissonance*. Stanford, CA: Stanford University Press.

Ford, J., & Ford, L. (2003). Conversations and the authoring of change. In: D. Holman & R. Thorpe (Eds.), *Management and Language* (pp. 141–156). London: Sage.

Fredman, G. (2004). *Transforming Emotion: Conversations in Counselling and Psychotherapy*. London: Whurr.

Gergen, K. J. (1994). *Realities and Relationships: Soundings in Social Construction*. Cambridge, MA: Harvard University Press.

Grønbæk, M. (2004). *Drømmen—fra tanke til handling* [The Dream—From Idea to Action]. Denmark: MG-UDVIKLING.

Harré, R., & Langenhove, L. V. (1999). *Positioning Theory*. Oxford: Blackwell.

Harré, R., & Moghaddam, F. M. (2004). *The Self and Others*. Westport, CT: Praeger.

Hermans, H. J. M., & Kempen, H. J. G. (1993). *The Dialogical Self: Meaning as Movement*. San Francisco, CA: Academic Press.

Kelly, G. A. (1955). *The Psychology of Personal Constructs, Vols. 1 & 2*. New York: W. W. Norton.

Kvale, S. (1996). *InterViews. An Introduction to Qualitative Research Interviewing*. London: Sage.

Langenhove, L. V., & Harré, R. (1999). Introducing positioning theory. In: R. Harré & L. V. Langenhove (Eds.), *Positioning Theory* (chap. 2). Oxford: Blackwell.

McNamee, S. (1992). Reconstructing identity: The communal construction of crisis. In: S. McNamee & K. Gergen (Eds.), *Therapy as Social Constructions*. London: Sage.

McNamee, S. , & Gergen, K. (Eds.) (1992). *Therapy as Social Constructions*. London: Sage.

McNamee, S., & Gergen, K. (1999). *Relational Responsibility*. Thousand Oaks, CA: Sage.

Parker, I. (1992). *Discourse Dynamics: Critical Analysis for Social and Critical Psychology*. London: Routledge.

Penman, R. (1992). Good theory and good practice: An argument in process. *Communication Theory, 2* (3): 234–250.

Riikonen, E. (1999). Inspiring dialogues and relational responsibility. In: S. McNamee & K. J. Gergen (Eds.), *Relational Responsibility* (chap. 13). Thousand Oaks, CA: Sage.

Sampson, E. (1993). *Celebrating the Other*. London: Harvester-Wheatsheaf.

Selvini Palazzoli, M., Boscolo, L., Cecchin, G., & Prata, G. (1980). Hypothesizing—circularity—neutrality: Three guidelines for the conductor of the session. *Family Process, 19*: 3–12.

Shotter, J. (1993). *Conversational Realities: Constructing Life through Language*. London: Sage.

Shotter, J. (2004). *On the Edge of Social Constructionism: "Withness" Thinking vs. "Aboutness" Thinking*. London: KCC Foundation.

Shotter, J., & Cunliffe, A. (2003). Managers as practical authors: Everyday conversations for action. In: D. Holman & R. Thorpe (Eds.), *Management and Language* (chap. 1). London: Sage.

Shotter, J., & Katz, A. (1999). Creating relational realities: Responsible responding to poetic "movements" and "moments". In: S. McNamee & K. J. Gergen, *Relational Responsibility* (chap. 14). Thousand Oaks, CA: Sage.

Ugazio, V. (1998). *Storie permesse e storie proibite*. Turin: Bollati Boringhieri.

White, M. (1991). *Deconstruction and Therapy*. Adelaide: Dulwich Centre Newsletter No. 3.

INDEX